ALIYAH
of the
HEART

David & Kirsten Hart

DEDICATION

We would like to dedicate this book to our son,
Ryan, who first taught us the word Aliyah. He has
shared his heart, time, effort, talents, and years to
helping people make Aliyah to Israel. Ryan, your
time spent living in Israel, and doing great works
for the Jewish people will never 'return void'.
In Numbers 24, Balaam prophesied from the Lord
about Israel, "May those who bless you be blessed
and those who curse you be cursed!"
Ryan, you have blessed Israel—walk in your
blessings.

CONTENTS

A Journey Of Faith
אמונה של מסע

Thousands of years ago, God called a man named Abraham to leave his familiar, and journey into a new land. There is something about stepping out beyond what we know into fresh and new adventures with him. New is who we are to you. Exciting is what we see and feel. Adventures are what he has planned.

Let us formally introduce ourselves. We are Dave and Kirsten Hart, the television hosts for Zola Levitt Presents. Over the months and years ahead we will be joining you in your homes via the television set or internet. Hopefully we will have a chance to meet face-to-face, or perhaps tour Israel and get to know you personally. But until we greet you in person, we'd like to tell you a bit of our story, and share with you our hearts for Israel.

We both grew up in Christian homes. I was raised on the East Coast in New York and New Jersey, and David was a West Coast boy. How can God bring together a girl from New Jersey and a boy from California? The same way he can unite Christians and those of the Jewish faith. On the outside we may seem different, but the similarities within bind us together.

We have been (very happily!) married since July 1990. We are blessed with two amazing sons, a Daughter-in-law, and a wonderful grandson and the most adorable Bella Rose Hart. We have loved and laughed through many seasons of life together. Now as empty-nesters, we embrace this open door with Zola Levitt Ministries. What an exciting time to be part of this phenomenal ministry.

God called our youngest son, Ryan, to work as a Video Production Specialist with the International Christian Embassy in 2016. Since Ryan's move to Jerusalem, Yeshua (the Hebrew name for Jesus) has been drawing us into a fresh relationship with the country of Israel with powerful momentum.

Just three weeks ago, we returned from leading music for a Mike Huckabee tour of the Holy Land. The freshness of our Israeli experience combined with our positions with this ministry is our assurance that God is doing a 'new thing' with us. We are humbled to be a small part of Jesus renewing people's hearts for his land and especially his people.

We are lovers of hummus, pita, falafel, and Israeli salad. We long for the peace of Shabbat in the Holy Land—which is a peace unlike any other.

We have a passion for Christians to know the significance of the Jewish feasts. We believe that Christians need to know and understand the depth of knowledge that only comes through embracing our Jewish foundations.

We've heard it said that 'one simply does not *go* to Israel, but rather God *calls* you there'. We feel called. Called to his land. Called to his people.

Don't feel bad if you have never heard the term 'Aliyah'. We didn't know the word until a few years ago, either. Aliyah is a special Hebrew term used in the Bible and is defined as 'the act of going up'.

The Jewish people would 'go up' to Jerusalem to worship at the Temple. They literally would go *up*. Jerusalem and the mountains of Zion are 2,474 feet high. While that might not seem high to those living in mountainous regions of the states—remember that the Jordan Valley in Israel (and specifically the Dead Sea region) is 1,410 feet *below* sea level. So in the days when transportation mostly consisted of walking, the people of the Bible most definitely had quite a hike to reach the Temple!

The Jordan Valley was (and greatly still is) the fertile farming region of the country, and where many people would both live and use as their 'highway' so to speak. The total elevation climb from the Dead Sea to the Temple Mount is (add the two together) 3,884 feet. Add that elevation climb with the possibility of walking all the way from the Northern area of Israel, and you've got quite a journey. A long *Aliyah*.

Aliyah can also mean the 'going up' of a man to

read the Torah. Since 1948, the term Aliyah has taken on a new meaning. It signifies those returning to the land of Israel to make it their new homeland. Those that are officially allowed to make Aliyah have to prove their Jewish heritage (usually through the mother's family line). Once their lineage is approved, there is a long process to complete in order to be an official Israeli citizen. It's not an easy process, but one that is increasing in numbers daily.

Aliyah is also a fulfillment of ancient scripture coming alive before our very eyes. In 70 A.D. the Jewish people were literally dispersed throughout the world. They no longer had a homeland. They were constantly foreigners in another land. In 1948, with a place to finally call their own, Jewish people from across the world started fulfilling the Ezekiel vision of the dry bones rising up and becoming alive again.

Isaiah talked about the great return of the people to Israel:

"He will raise a banner for the nations and gather the exiles of Israel; He will assemble the scattered people of Judah from the four corners of the earth."
(Isaiah 11:12)

There are many other Aliyah scriptures, but I want to explain how a gentile couple like we are can even apply the term to our lives.

In 2008, I discovered that I had been adopted, and I never knew that fact about my life. Yes, it was an unbelievable journey—and it still is. Years later (after we had made trips to Israel), I decided to do a

DNA test. I was hoping for some Jewish blood in me. When I got my results back in the mail, I discovered no Jewish DNA. I was disappointed. I would never have the opportunity or open door to make Aliyah to Israel.

I couldn't physically move to the country as a citizen, *but* I knew my heart was definitely there. That's where the title for this book came from. If I couldn't rightfully and legally move to Israel, I knew at least that my heart belonged there.

Unfortunately, many American churches don't understand the significance of serving and following a Jewish savior. We, the church, have been missing out on so many deep spiritual 'links' by not understanding our Jewish roots. My heart's desire with this book is that you, too, will *make an Aliyah* of the heart with me. May your heart be drawn to the Jewish people, and God's Holy Land.

The Land Of Promise
הההבטחה ארץ

We are beginning a new journey with all of you through this book, and we couldn't be more excited. Hopefully you have seen our faces on Zola Levitt Presents. It is such a huge honor to be a small part of carrying on what Zola started so many years ago. We, too, have a heart for Israel, and God's chosen people. What an incredible journey we are now on. And you are part of our journey—our new friend.

God has been drawing people to his land since the beginning. There's just something about that land. God could have chosen any spot on this beautiful earth for his people, but for some reason, he looked at that small land with natural springs, fertile soil, and desert climates and knew it was where he wanted his people to dwell.

He would call those listening to come. He called

to Adam. Adam responded and had a relationship. He called to Noah to build an ark, and Noah responded and built an ark. Then God called to Abram.

In Genesis 12, God calls out to a man named Abram. And Abram listened. *"Go from your country, your people and your father's household to the land I will show you. I will make you into a great nation, and I will bless you; I will make your name great, and you will be a blessing. I will bless those who bless you, and whoever curses you I will curse; and all peoples on earth will be blessed through you."* (Genesis 12: 1-3 NIV)

Most of you can probably recite this verse from heart. Abram was seventy-five when he heard God's voice, and responded to the new call on his life. God had the land planned out before time began. Abram heard God's voice, and started a new journey that would change the world.

I wonder how many others God has called to his land, but they didn't listen to his voice. It's in the listening. God is still calling those who will listen, to go to his Promised Land. Perhaps he is calling you to Israel, too. I know he has called us. Just a few months ago, we were honored to walk in that land prepared by God himself for his people.

We were sitting at the top of Mount of Beatitudes (also known as Mt. Eremos), listening to a teaching about communion. All of us on the tour were about to partake of this sacrament, when I turned my head to the right to gaze over the Sea of Galilee. This was the land that Yahweh himself designed specifically for his people. Yeshua, the *word* of God spoke it into being. It was *his* land. And it is a beautiful land.

The leaders were giving instructions about how we would proceed with the sacraments, and all I could think about what the fact that out of all the continents, islands, and various lands on this planet, that God himself picked out these 8,019 square miles of terrain all for himself.

I pondered these thoughts as the sun was starting to slowly descend over the Arbel Cliffs. Yeshua himself, the speaker of Creation, looked out over this land and said, "It is good".

To think that two-thousand years ago, the very eyes of God-become-flesh used human eyes to see his creation of Israel. The Land that Yahweh created specifically for his people is like none other. He could have chosen the Alps in Switzerland, England with its majestic ocean cliffs, or perhaps even the islands of Hawaii. All beautiful locations. Instead, he picked this land that sweeps along the Mediterranean, has desert oasis spots, and fertile soil ready to grow everything and anything needed for survival.

Why do the Harts love Israel? How many books can I fill? What other land is there that still looks like it did when Abraham walked its paths, yet is on the cutting edge of technology? Everywhere you look in Jerusalem, there is building. And every building is a physical fulfillment of prophecy. It *didn't* happen. It is present tense happen*ing*—all across this tiny nation.

Nowhere else in this world can you physically personally touch ancient prophetic words coming to life. I don't say this about many places, but there is an electricity in the very air of that country. The ground you walk on may be filled with wildflowers, or ancient stones, but it truly is holy ground. Set apart. Destined for a Kingdom to be ruled once again by Yeshua as the King of Kings and Lord of Lords in an earthly reign.

You're reading this because you are interested in Israel. I would encourage you to come see this land for yourself. Even if you journeyed to Israel before, you won't believe the changes that can take place even in a year's time. Archeological discoveries are being unearthed as we speak.

Yeshua is rapidly revealing himself through ancient stones and sites throughout the land. This land that he loves so very much is teaming with his beloved people. They are truly coming from the north, south, east, and the west! They are once again inhabiting the land that Yeshua spoke into being, and that he looked upon and loved with his very eyes.

On our last tour, there was a woman who was celebrating her 50th tour to the Holy Land. She shared that every single time, her experience is different, and she learns something new. That's because that land is...*holy*, set apart.

We would love for you to join us in seeing what is currently taking place in Israel. If you have never taken a journey to the Holy Land—come! Your life and outlook will change for the better. We know. It's happened to us. If you've been, you know that every trip is different, and the knowledge gained grows with every single tour.

Through reading this book, my heart's desire is that you will fall in love (or more in love) with your Creator, your Jewish Messiah, and the land God deemed holy. The chapters aren't long, and they are taken from articles I have written for the monthly publication from Zola Levitt Presents. The chapters don't follow an exact sequence, so feel free to skip around if you want.

May your heart be also drawn to finding out more truths about God's heart, and his love for all people.

Here we are standing on the walls of the Old City of
Jerusalem. There is a walk along the upper part of
the inside of the wall, called The Ramparts. It's a
fascinating and beautiful hike with a lot of steps, but
it's really cool. We stopped here, because behind us
(with the grey domed roof) is the Upper Room.

Below the Upper Room, is the supposed tomb of
King David.

We're walking the streets of the Old City with one of our Zola Tours. All of the stone in Jerusalem is 'Jerusalem stone', and is a pale limestone that has been used since ancient times. For the past 3,000 years, this is the stone that has been used for roads and buildings throughout Israel.

Notice the etched Hebrew above the walkway. You may already know this, but Hebrew is written and read right-to-left.

Relax And Let Go
ולנוח להירגע

We recently purchased a small lake cabin here, in Branson, Missouri. We're anticipating hours of kayaking and paddle boarding, and everything that goes along with lake life! We have two grandchildren now, so we need to do our best to stay healthy and in shape.

Not too long ago, we were on another body of water, The Dead Sea. People say they swim in the Dead Sea, but it's an entirely different 'swim' than in a traditional lake. If you haven't been in the Dead Sea, you need to put it on your personal bucket list. In my humble opinion, it's truly a natural wonder of our world. To get the most out of your Dead Sea experience, you have to do one thing: relax.

When we were there in March on our Zola Tour, I took a look around at those in the water. There were two types of people: the standers, and the floaters. The standers are an interesting bunch. Most of them have traveled across the ocean to experience Israel and this body of water, but they remain standing, rather than to float. Yes, some of them have applied the world-famous mud to their skin, but their trust level in the ability of the water to keep them afloat is limited. So limited, that they miss out on one of the greatest experiences in the Holy Land.

Then there is my group: the floaters. My people 'get it'. My people swim/float all the way out to the boundary rope. Was it deep at the boundary rope? No idea. Why? Because you simply can't go beneath the surface to the bottom. The floaters bring a newspaper or paperback book to read, while enjoying this anti-gravity adventure. There's a simple trick, if you will, to getting the most out of your Dead Sea experience. You have to relax and let go. Trust the water. What I figured out watching people in March? Lots of people have a hard time with trusting.

"You literally just need to get in the water, and lean back. Trust that the water will hold you. When you completely relax, the water will keep your body in a perfect float position" I told the people on our tour. Those that trusted, got the treat of a lifetime. Those that struggled with relaxing and trusting ended up face down in the mineral water. You don't want that. *"Relax and let go"* was my encouraging phrase that day.

The 'standers' enjoyed standing, I suppose. But you can stand in any body of water. To float in the

Dead Sea, in my opinion, is just a glimpse of Peter walking on the water towards Jesus on the Sea of Galilee. Peter had to completely trust Jesus.

Walking on water wasn't something that he was used to. It was unnatural. It went against the laws of physics. Just as floating in the Dead Sea. "But I'm not a swimmer" I heard from so many. "There isn't any swimming involved! You won't believe how amazing it is!" I encouraged.

If Peter had called out to Jesus, "But I'm not a person that walks on water!" he would have missed one of the greatest experiences of his life. He had to trust that Jesus (Yeshua) would take care of him. Peter had to look beyond the known physical elements and trust that something beyond the natural would take place. Jesus gave him the walk of his life…until he lost sight of Jesus, and focused in on the water beneath his feet.

In a world full of trust issues, the one thing we can rely on is that Jesus will always be there for us. The more we trust in him, the easier our struggle.

Psalm 56:3 *"When I am afraid, I put my trust in you."*

Proverbs 3:5 *"Trust in the LORD with all your heart and lean not on your own understanding."*

Relax, let go, and see how the Lord will keep you afloat.

The Dead Sea is one of my absolute favorite spots. My hands were full of mud, even though it was a rainy day on this visit. The mud is incredibly healing. Even ancient Cleopatra had the mud from the Dead Sea as a beauty treatment! When you go on a tour with us, you will find me running to get into the water asap!

Dave and I floating 'swimming' in the Dead Sea.
You really can't sink! One of the most fun
experiences ever.

Ephesus Insight

תובנה אפסוס

Insight moments, to me, are priceless. May I mention another one? If you keep reading, I suppose that means, 'yes'. This insight actually happened in ancient Ephesus on our Zola Levitt Greek cruise. (I'm telling you, you *must* go at least once in your lifetime). First of all, ancient Ephesus is completely amazing.

Ephesus streets were *solid marble*. Only 1/10th of the city has been unearthed, and it literally took us all day to explore. One of the spots we learned about was the ancient public bathroom.

As we were walking through the majestic streets and buildings of this enormous city, our guide led us to an area of solid marble that was, literally, the public restroom. Thirty-six people could use the 'facility' at the same time. Their technology was so far advanced, and although I understand it might not be so proper to write about a public toilet, it was fascinating to learn about.

My 'ah-ha' moment came when our guide was telling us that if you were wealthy, you could hire a slave to 'clean' you after you were finished. "In ancient times, slaves were paid to take a long stick with an attached sponge dipped in vinegar to clean of the 'participant'. It's the same stick that was given to Jesus when he was on the cross."

"A jar of wine vinegar was there, so they soaked a sponge in it, put the sponge on a stalk of the hyssop plant, and lifted it to Jesus' lips." (John 19:29)

That revelation took my breath away. It was all I could think about for the rest of the day. When Yeshua HaMashiach (the Messiah in Hebrew), our Savior, was on the cross and thirsty, one of the soldiers took a tool used to clean someone after they used a public toilet, and put it to his mouth.

I've read and heard the words Jesus spoke on the cross my whole life, but I never understood why they put a vinegar-soaked sponge to his lips. Even in his very last moments of human life, our Lord endured complete humiliation in order to redeem the world.

Ancient Ephesus is a place that Paul stayed, and as I'm sure you realize, the book of Ephesus was written to those living in that city. I understand that in a book about Israel, the fact that I am commenting on ruins in modern-day Turkey may seem odd. But the steps of Paul, and where he took the gospel all originates (obviously) in Israel, and with our Jewish Messiah.

The insight of Jesus on the cross, and the sponge that was lifted to his lips will stay with me forever, thanks to our visit to ancient Ephesus.

The 'famous' discovered public toilets in Ancient Ephesus.

From The Realms Of Glory
התהילה ממלכות

"You have to see them with Sprit eyes." I have heard that line from people who claim that they have actually seen a 'live' angel. And I literally heard someone say to me, "They're in the back of the sanctuary. Can't you *see* them?" *I COULDN'T SEE THEM!* And I'm telling you, I *really* wanted to see the angels standing in the back!

Have *you* ever seen an angel? I'm always kind of fascinated by the supernatural realm. I know that it's simply another dimension that we can't see with our limited human minds and eyes. We were created 'a little lower' than the angels (Psalm 8:5).

There are things happening all around us that we physically can't see. But sometimes. *Some times* that curtain is temporarily lifted, and we humans can catch a glimpse into the world just beyond our senses. God gives us a few moments to see beyond our everyday, to experience where he daily dwells. The shepherds in Bethlehem experienced that awe and wonder on the night Jesus was born.

Honestly, could you *imagine* what the shepherds that night experienced? There previously had been angel sightings in the scriptures—but usually with just *one* angel. In the book of Luke, chapter one, starting with verse twenty-six, we are told that "In the sixth month, God sent the angel Gabriel to Nazareth, a town in Galilee, to a virgin pledged to be married to a man named Joseph, a descendant of David. The virgin's name was Mary. The angel went to her and said, 'Greetings, you who are highly favored! The Lord is with you'."

Imagine being Mary, and seeing an angel for the first time, then receiving this (almost) unbelievable news. Yet that was just *one* angel. The shepherds saw a *multitude* of the heavenly host. And I'm assuming that's a lot of angels.

So just how many angels *are* in a *host*? The Greek word for host (stratia) refers to "the heavenly bodies, stars of heaven--so called on account of their number and order." The heavenly host present at Jesus' birth were so numerous they were compared to the stars. Who can count the stars, much less number and order them, other than God?

The King James Version translates Luke 2:13 to say "a multitude of the heavenly host." Let's do the math. If one heavenly host is as numerous as the stars, how many is a *multitude* of heavenly host? Can't count that high.

In Genesis 12, when God was telling Abraham

about all the decedents he will have, God told Abraham, "Look up at the sky and count the stars-- if indeed you can count them." Only God can count how many stars and galaxies there are—just as only God could have counted the hosts of angels that were praising God in the Bethlehem sky.

I have been in arenas where there were thousands of people. I know what 'thousands' looks and sounds like. I have never been in a setting with tens of thousands nor hundreds of thousands, yet alone multitude of a 'host'. If the heavens opened up enough for *multitudes* of *hosts* to be seen, I'm thinking there was a *huge* opening in the sky at that moment. Surely the shepherds out in the field weren't the only ones out and about that night, yet *all those angels* were only seen by a few chosen shepherds.

I'm sure all of Heaven was rejoicing as they got to see the unveiling of God's plan for redemption. I know the Bible teaches us that "With the Lord a day is like a thousand years, and a thousand years are like a day" (II Peter 3:8), but still. The angels had waited *forever* to be able to make all of these exciting announcements. What anticipation!

The time had come. And to those shepherds that were on duty with the sheep that night, wow. Talk about being in the right place at the right time!

Was December 25th the exact night when the angels announced Messiah's birth? Probably not. Are we all celebrating his birth on a pagan holiday? Yes. Do many of our traditions come from pagan beliefs and practices? Yes. The more I learn about factual Bible history, the more it bothers me that we have so diluted the Gospel message with traditions so far removed from the truth about the birth of Christ.

Although the exact date of Yeshua's birth isn't given to us, we still have so many wonderful details about that blessed night. The night that the long-awaited Prince of Peace was born Heaven touched earth. Humble shepherds saw angels with their eyes, and caught a glimpse of the heavens.

We aren't told the name of the angel that announced the birth of Jesus to the shepherds. But I am sure when the heavens opened up, they were *all there*! And those angels didn't look like the little cherub figurines we have sitting around our houses on little shelves. They're strong warriors. In the Old Testament, Daniel tells us of an angel he saw that had 'eyes of fire'.

No wonder one of the first words an angel speaks is, "Fear not". They're strong, tough beings. The whole Bethlehem sky was filled with those beings proclaiming, "Glory to God in the highest, And on earth peace among men with whom He is pleased."

And that was just the *beginning* of the first day of Jesus' life. What a baby announcement!

Bethlehem (the word in Hebrew means house of bread!) is a city that we visit on our tours. While it is now under Palestinian rule, and feels very different from Jerusalem, it's still remarkable to visit the famous 'Shepherds field', which is the area where shepherds 2,000+ years ago would tend their sheep.

This is the famous statue/fountain at Shepherd's Field in Bethlehem. There are actual ancient caves you can go in that were caves used in the time of Jesus. On our tours, we always go into one of these caves, and sing Christmas carols.

A 'modern day' shepherd at Nazareth village, who literally tends the sheep and goats on a daily basis. Nazareth village is a spot in Nazareth owned by our Branson friend, Sherry Herschend.

A Cup Of Chai
חיים כוס

I never knew chai was a drink option until just a few years ago. I've never been a coffee drinker, but when I discovered chai tea, I knew I liked it. Sweet with a little spice. It's a wonderful combination of tea, cream, cinnamon, cloves, nutmeg, and even peppercorns! Apparently this drink goes back thousands of years. And to think that I didn't even know it existed until just recently.

Another chai I recently learned about comes from our beloved Israel. I grew up singing along with the famous actor Topol (his given name was interestingly enough *Chaim* Topol) as he sang and portrayed the role of Tevye in Fiddler on the Roof. We watched it every time it came on the TV. And to be honest, I usually fell asleep on the couch before it was over. It's a three hour movie, plus commercials! My favorite song in the musical was L'chai-im. (My second favorite was Matchmaker.)

To life! To life! L'chai-im!
L'chai-im, l'chai-im, to life!
If you've been lucky, then Monday was
No worse than Sunday was,
Drink l'chai-im, to life.

From watching Fiddler on the Roof all those years, I obviously picked up that L'chai-im was a toast *to life*! It wasn't until this most recent trip to the Holy Land, that I discovered the true beauty of *chai*. It is my favorite Hebrew word and symbol made from the Hebrew letters Het and Yud.

Our youngest son Ryan lives in Jerusalem, and is the Video Production Specialist for the International Christian Embassy. Before our last tour group arrived in Israel, we had five days to just spend with our boy.

We wanted to see where he lived, where he went to the movies, where he shopped for groceries, and what his normal everyday life was like. (Side note? The movie theater we went to with him in Jerusalem was *way cooler* than any movie theater we've ever been to in the States! It most definitely is *not* a backwards or third world country!)

Thursday evening, as we were sitting in our apartment together, I read that to be at the Western Wall just as Shabbat starts on Fridays is quite an experience. So I made the suggestion that the three of us (David, Ryan, and myself) journey to the Old

37

City late Friday afternoon. Ryan had not yet experienced bringing in Shabbat at The Wall (*Ha-kotel*), so he was excited to experience this event with us.

As we walked through the Dung Gate into the Old City, I realized (once again!) that we Evangelical Christian Americans are missing out on amazing Jewish traditions. The energy and excitement was thick and pulsating. I've never experienced anything like it.

The singing, dancing, joyous shouts of praise and thanksgiving reverberated throughout the Kotel. IDF soldiers were circling up, holding hands, and dancing with joy. Songs thanking Elohim for another week of *chai,* (life!) were being sung in languages from many nations! Young boys making their Bar Mitzvah journey were seen throughout. The joy of life was tangible.

I turned to Ryan and whispered, "It's so sad that we don't have *anything* like this in the United States." He, with a wisdom beyond his twenty-three years of life replied, "But with this kind of chai, is also great sorrow."

The Jewish people have walked through thousands of years of persecution, yet their gratitude for life, and the rejoicing at the beginning of Shabbat was more than I ever imagined. Why don't we in America rejoice like the Israelis on the eve of Shabbat? Have we not walked through enough intense sorrow as a people and nation to appreciate the simplicity of living through another week, to appreciate the coming day of rest?

Come to think of it, taking a Sabbath/Shabbat is

very un-American. We don't rest here. We have a hard time stopping everything to simply shut it all down, and follow through with a time of quiet and gratefulness.

Before leaving Israel on our most recent trip, I bought a sterling silver necklace with two sterling charms. One was the Star of David, and the other, the Hebrew symbol for chai. If nothing else, I wanted to remember the extremes of the Jewish people.

With great sorrow (the Star of David worn in the Holocaust), comes the ability to recognize great chai. It just may be impossible to experience extreme chai without walking through extreme pain.

When you have your next cup of warm chai tea, will you remember the Hebrew meaning of the word, and rejoice that you have life? If you don't have this life and joy that I am writing about, I pray that today would be the day that you would be ready to let Yeshua/Jesus into your life. For it truly is only through Him, that you can experience abundant life. It's simple. Ask for forgiveness, ask that He would become the Lord of your life, and thank Him for the gift of eternal salvation.

"I am come that they might have life (*chai*), and
that they might have it more abundantly."
(John 10:10)

DAVID & KIRSTEN HART

This is my favorite drink in Israel. I do love their chai tea, but this was actually a mug of Israeli hot chocolate. It is incredible. You pretty much get a coffee mug full of warm, steamed milk, and at the bottom is some of the world's best chocolate. You simply stir it all together. Hard to describe how delicious this is!

I bought myself these two charms to remind myself of the two extremes of Israeli people. The great life (chai), and the great sorrow they have walked through. This is one of my favorite necklaces from Israel.

Read Galatians, Friends
הגלטיים את לקרוא, חברים

I was simply scrolling through my Facebook page. Grinning at photos of friend's children, smiling at funny posts, when I read an interesting status. It was something written by apparently someone I attended college with, although I didn't remember this gentleman. His status read, "Why do so many Christians want to be Jews? Read Galatians, friends."

Well, that intrigued me. Probably not in the best way, though. I started reading through all of the responses. I couldn't help it. I had to write a response, so I did. "Jesus was 100% Jewish. Maybe to be more like Christ?" Then it began. Backlash time. The first response to my comment was, "GALATIONS!" To which I responded, "One book? How about all the rest?"

That pretty much started it. I was in deep. "What book on this side of the cross tells Christians to act like Jews?!!!" "Are you being serious or playing the devil's advocate, Kirsten?!! OMGosh!!!" "Read Galatians and feel the passion of the Jewish believer against Gentiles being bewitched into acting like Jews and get back to me."

At this point, I probably should have turned off my social media, but I didn't. I kept reading, and was intrigued by the various responses I was reading. So where do we, as believers draw the line? Can Messianic believers in Yeshua partake of 'rituals' that Christians aren't allowed to do?

Where is the offensive/non-offensive line? How do Christian believers learn what we can and can't do? If a Gentile believer wants to wear a prayer shawl, is that allowed, or wrong? Can we partake in only certain feasts?

Yes, I am writing this as a Gentile believer that was raised in Christian churches her whole life, but now has a newfound love for Israel and God's chosen people.

What part of the original law handed to Moses do we follow and obey? Can Christians pick and choose which aspects of the Law we follow, or are we "free" from all of it?

We want the financial bounty of the tithe, but won't adhere to keeping Shabbat. It's almost like "this one we want", "that one doesn't apply to us". Pick and choose. Yes, no…no, no, yes. A sorting through. We keep and follow the Ten Commandments (Christians like those), but we don't feel the need to keep the one about Shabbat.

Are believers in Yeshua free of all the written law? Is it only about the 'new Law written on our hearts'?

Now getting back to that original Facebook post. *"Why do so many Christians want to be Jews? Read Galatians, friends!"* Speaking for David and me, we don't need to be of Jewish heritage (but wouldn't that be wonderful!), rather we embrace that which is our foundational heritage of faith. Our Lord and Savior was the best Jew that ever lived. He followed the law perfectly.

We are told that Yeshua/Jesus "Grew in wisdom and stature, and in favor with God and man." (Luke 2:52) This tells us that he observed and followed the very law He gave to Moses. Yeshua, the *Word* of God, spoke the law into existence. He made it. He followed it. He fulfilled it.

Perhaps we are not *under* the same Old Testament laws, as Gentile believers. Does that mean we cut off any and everything Old Testament? Yeshua himself observed all of the feasts. I don't believe He ever said, "You are not to observe the Feasts anymore". In fact, the observance of communion is part of the Passover Feast! He told the Disciples, "Do this in remembrance of me." (Luke 22:19) But in churches, we only observe the new 'communion cup' of the feast.

Christians 'wanting to be Jews'? Perhaps these Christians see the beauty, significance, and actual relevance of the Feasts and Laws given to God's people. We long for the depth of relationship that Yahweh has had with His people since His promises to Abraham. We realize that Yeshua came *for His people*. Let's face the truth, Gentiles weren't *His* people...like it or not.

Perhaps some of you reading this have either grown up Jewish, or studied Judaism for years. There are also those who are just now embracing and recognizing the significance of finding out more about the Jewish roots of their faith. Even in 'our' name, it's interesting that I was always taught that to be Christian meant being Christ-like. Well, to be truly Christ-like, we would be Jewish, yes?

The beauty of all of this? We are on our own journeys to be more like Christ. Isn't that the goal we *all have in common?* I'm thankful that in Matthew 22:37-40, Jesus Himself told us what He desired of those who followed Him. "'Love the Lord your God with all your heart and with all your soul and with all your mind.' This is the first and greatest commandment. And the second is like it: 'Love your neighbor as yourself.' All the Law and the Prophets hang on these two commandments."

Sometimes it's way more simple than we think. I'd love to know how *you* feel! Are you a Jewish believer in Yeshua? A Christian believer? Can we criss-cross what we all do in remembrance, celebration of, and worship of our Savior? Let me know!

Breakfast With The King
המלך עם בוקר ארוחת

As you can probably assume from reading this book, I love the land of Israel. You could also assume that I have many favorite spots in the Holy Land.

I want to focus on a small patch of land on the northwestern coast of Lake Kinneret (the Sea of Galilee). This freshwater lake is one of the most peaceful spots on the planet Earth. It's named *Kinneret* (a derivative of the Hebrew word for a harp, *kinnor*) because its shape resembles that of an Old Testament harp! It is also the location for the majority of Jesus' earthly ministry. Of all the miracles that transpired, my favorite revolves around a simple breakfast of fish and bread.

I'm literally smiling as I write this, because I just love how Jesus simultaneously was the glorious risen King of Kings, yet an unrecognizable (at first) man cooking fish over a fire next to the lake. In the twenty-first chapter of the book of John, we read this wonderful reunion with His disciples.

"I'm going out to fish" are the words recorded in John that Simon Peter spoke to the disciples. The disciples had just walked through the most traumatic time in their lives with the crucifixion and resurrection of Messiah. Their lives had been turned upside down, yet it seemed as if life was back to normal. Fishing—the original trade of many of the disciples—was what they 'returned to' after arriving back to the Galilee area from Jerusalem.

The disciples had just experienced the miraculous. Jesus *risen from the dead*, yet everyday life continued on. Time to catch some fish. Normalcy. It wasn't long before, that they experienced thousands of people being fed (only a few hundred feet from their present fishing spot) with a simple fish and loaf of bread. Were they perhaps reminiscing together about that time? "*Remember when....?*"

They had a whole night (apparently) out on the water together, but zero fish caught. Then sunrise, and the lone outline of a man on the shore, "Friends, haven't you any fish?" Where do I begin with how I love that comment from our Lord?

First off, Yeshua uses the word *friends*. Those out on the fishing boat *were* his friends: Messiah's dearest and closest human friends. They had seen first-hand miracle upon miracle, and yet most of them 'scattered' at the time of Christ's crucifixion—especially Peter who publically denied

Him three times. Yet the risen Savior of the world still calls out to them, "Friends..."

You've got to know that Jesus was smiling and had a bit of tongue in cheek humor (if you will) with asking them if they had caught any fish. These were the men who, first hand, were part of fish multiplying and appearing supernaturally. No fish caught that night? Those fishermen knew that there were fish to be caught...and multiplied.

Then, as only our Savior could say and do, "Throw your net on the right side of the boat and you will find some." As if the boat span of a few feet could make a difference in catching fish? But it did.

The risen King, once again, proved his fish multiplying skills. To be honest, if I were Jesus (which I realize I am not), I would probably have called out to the Disciples something more like, "You've been *out all night*, and not one single fish? *Seriously*? Don't you guys get how to tap into the miraculous yet? Three *years* you've been part of seeing miracles, and you still don't get it? I'm so disappointed in all of you!"

But then, like the Savior he is, Yeshua himself performed yet another fish miracle for his best friends. And my favorite *favorite* part? God himself, in resurrected form, cooked a breakfast over a campfire for his disciples. A simple breakfast. He could have prepared a feast resembling the Marriage Supper in Heaven, but Jesus kept it basic.

I bet that bread and fish was the best tasting breakfast those disciples had ever tasted. I can't even imagine. Did Jesus kneed the bread himself?

Did angels prepare the bread and deliver it to him? Did that food just *poof* instantly appear on the fire? Did Jesus catch that fish out of the Sea of Galilee with his bare hands? Did he use a fishing net that morning?

Jesus told Peter, "Bring some of the fish you caught". (Ever wonder where church potlucks originated?) The conversation that followed around that campfire changed the world. The disciples, and Peter in particular, that morning had a fresh call on their lives—and it all started with an unexpected cookout. Simplistic, yet life-changing. That's my Savior.

Our Yeshua, still today is calling out to all of us, "*Friends…*" He's the exalted King who triumphed over death, yet still a Savior who wants to cook some fish and bread over a campfire. I love him. I love his ways.

"Come after me, and I will make you fishers of men..."

This is what they call a 'Jesus boat'. It's a boat used today on the Sea of Galilee that resembles a fisherman-type of boat used in Jesus' day. When we are on tour in the Galilee area, we always take an hour long cruise on one of these boats. The peace of the lake/sea? It's as if you can cut it with a knife. I'd love for you to experience that kind of peace.

David took this early morning photo off the balcony of our hotel room in Tiberias. We're not necessarily early morning people, but this photo was totally worth the early morning alarm! Another 'Jesus boat' on the Sea of Galilee.

It's All Greek To Us
όλα μας είναι ελληνικά

On Zola Levitt Presents, we weekly invite you to take the adventure of a lifetime to Israel. We mention Greece, and the Greek cruise, too. But I wanted to share with you the TOP TEN reasons David and I think you should go to *Greece* with us.

#1
See the Acropolis, Parthenon, and Mars Hill for yourself. They're magnificent. Pictures don't do these spots justice. Mars Hill is the place (and it is actually a *hill*) where Paul preached to the Athenians about the 'Unknown God' (Acts 17:22-31). Mars Hill is a few steps away from the Acropolis where there were temples built to many different Greek gods. You will be able to stand in the same exact spot Paul did! Climbing up to the

Parthenon and seeing all of Athens spread out
before you is breathtaking.

#2
The sidewalks in Athens are made out of marble.
This was a fascinating fact to us. Even the sewer

grates are *marble*. This might not be a life changing reason to go to Greece, but if I add the fact that the gorgeous hotel that we stay in is literally feet away from the famous changing of the guards, and combine that with the knowledge that you can see the guards 24/7, well, that makes #2 a good combo.

#3

I and II Corinthians were books written to the people in Corinth, Greece. You, yourself, will have the opportunity to walk through the beautiful old city of Corinth. With its sprawling views of the Ionian Sea, and the fact that you can literally walk where Paul himself taught the Corinthians, you won't be disappointed. Look up to see the Acrocorinth, a medieval Crusader fortress, which actually has gates dating back to the 4th century BC. Bring your walking shoes, because we get to explore this ancient expansive site.

#4

As if the days of seeing Athens and Corinth weren't enough, we get to hop on a cruise ship through the Aegean Sea. The sapphire waters of the Aegean will make you want to stand on the boat deck and stare at the water endlessly. When you tire of that activity, the food will be waiting for you. Our favorite was the Greek BBQ night on the Lido deck. The endless amounts of grilled meats, salads, sides, and *desserts*? Worth the whole trip. The ship's cabins? Roomy. The dining room cuisine? Exquisite. Be sure to join David and I on the upper Lido deck whenever we approach a port, or leave the port. We'll show you the best spots for great viewing.

#5

Ephesus. Not only did Paul write to the Ephesians, but he was also a resident of the ancient metropolis. Only 10% of Ancient Ephesus has been uncovered...and it took us a whole day to explore the city. I could write volumes about our experience there.

Honestly, we had no idea the magnitude of this city. Streets? Solid marble. Frescos painted on the walls thousands of years ago? Still marvelously visible and vibrant. The endless mosaic 'floor rugs' made me seriously reconsider the floors we currently have in our condo. Not sure if I could recreate the intricate mosaic designs we saw in the Terrace Houses, but I sure thought about it.

Prepare to be amazed there. And if you're a cat lover, apparently bringing cat food to feed the Ephesus 'street cats' is a thing people do.

#6

We get to go to Patmos. *Patmos*! We actually get to journey into the actual cave where the Apostle John had the revelation, and 'penned' the words of the last book in the Bible. There's a crack in the ceiling of the cave that apparently happened when the voice of the Lord spoke to John.

After our exploration of this site, we will meet as a group for Praise and Worship. Nothing like singing Revelation Song together, steps from where it all took place.

#7

You can use U.S. dollars and credit cards throughout Greece, but it's really fun to have Euros. I'm a grown woman, but still think that using foreign currency is cool.

#8

"It looks like there's snow on top of the mountains. How is there snow on a Greek Island??" (Me, on our approach to Santorini). I soon realized that 'snow' was actually the myriad of pure white Santorini houses.

There's a reason Santorini is one of the most beloved Greek Islands. Its beauty is unparalleled. After our guided bus tour to the town of Oia (if you don't like heights, sit in an aisle seat!), we are free to explore the majestic cliff-side village on our own.

When the shop merchants offer you a SantoNut, accept it. These sesame seed and honey covered peanuts are delicious. We munched from the bag we bought throughout the rest of our tour!

#9

A sunset on the island of Mykonos. Can a Zola Tour to Greece be romantic? Yes. Mykonos at sunset shall prove that correct.

#10

After debarkation, we jump on our tour bus, and literally head right to the airport, and board our plane for the Holy Land. Because, on a Zola Tour, it just keeps getting better and better.

We'll save a seat on the bus, and a cabin on the cruise ship for you!

The colors of the famous city of Oia on Santorini is breathtaking.

Save Us!

אותנו הצל

If I had been a Jewish woman when Yeshua was born, I know what I would have been looking for in a Messiah. I would have wanted a military leader to save us from the oppression of the Romans, and more specifically someone just like Judah Maccabee, please.

We so easily jump on the Jewish people in Jesus' day for not accepting and recognizing Yeshua ben Yosef (Jesus son of Joseph) as the Messiah. But if I were to be honest, I think I would have had my doubts, too.

I just finished yet another course in the Institute of Jewish-Christian Studies which is offered through our ministry. (If you haven't gone through the Institute courses, I highly recommend you do so.) Course #8 is titled 'Between The Testaments'.

Growing up in the church, I've always viewed those roughly 400 years as 'silent' ones. Nothing much happened in Israel or to the Israelites. People lived life day in and day out in a sort of 'hum-drum' way for four-hundred years. There wasn't a prophet of God. There weren't any books written. It was as if there was a silent stand-still in the Biblical realm. Or so we were taught.

Sunday school lessons taught us that *finally*, after the whole intertestamental period, God once again revealed himself through bringing forth his son in the town of Bethlehem. The 'silence' had been broken. And, yes, in a way that's true of what the Bible most of us have in our hands tells us. Ahhhh, but those 'silent years' weren't actually so silent.

The years after Malachi and before Matthew found the Israelites in some of the most hostile and critical periods of survival as a people and a nation. Antiochus IV Epiphanes sought to destroy the Jewish faith, and to take the Jewish people down to their knees.

Through the destruction of the Temple, and the utter desecration of all that was holy to the Israelites, there arose a Jewish leader, a savior for the people. If you have studied anything about Hanukkah (the Feast of Dedication), you know this story.

Disgusted with the Greek influence, horrific rule of Antiochus, and the abomination of desolation in the Temple, there arose a man by the name of Mattathias ben (son of) Johanan. Mattathias, a Jewish priest started a revolt, which was carried out by his son, Judah. Judah had the nickname 'the Hammer', because his blows to the Syrians hit so strong.

Judah was a warrior savior for the Jewish people. With a strong hand and keen military wisdom, Judah defeated Antiochus and his armies. Thought to possibly be the promised Messiah, the nation of Israel rejoiced with the victory that Judah and the Maccabees (his followers) brought to Jerusalem. The Temple, under Judah, was once again restored and worship re-established.

For years and years, the Feast of Dedication was celebrated by the Jewish people. Stories of how God used the Maccabees to overthrow the Syrians was taught from generation to generation. Then the Romans decided to conquer Israel.

This God-promised land has always been a place for conquering. The Romans, in 63 BC, decided it was time for them to conquer and rule in Israel. Once again, tyranny against the Jewish people became part of everyday life. The Hebrew people once again were looking for the new Judah Maccabee to save them from oppression. An aggressive revolt saved the Jewish people from Antiochus. If it worked then, it would work again.

Then a baby was born. An innocent, helpless, infant was God's answer to tyranny. That's not the way it worked with people like the Romans. A strong, powerful hand was the only way to overcome such cruelty. If I had seen my family slaughtered by Roman soldiers riding through my village, I, too would have scoffed at the idea that a tiny baby born of two Nazarites would be God's answer for his people.

Because we have the hindsight of living when we do, we can see how God's plan was perfect, although different from what the Jewish people were expecting. A warrior/messiah who heals through words, instead of someone whose nickname was 'the Hammer' was vastly in contradiction to what had worked in the past. And on top of Yeshua not being a military leader, he did things that were seemingly contrary to the Torah. He questioned the authorities, and went against the grain.

Even his disciples were anxious for the 'Warrior Messiah' to take his rightful place in leadership. The Kingdom of God was thought to be a kingdom that would forcibly overtake the Romans. Up until the very end, his followers waited for their 'Hammer' to strike the authorities. Dying on a cross was an unexpected way for a Messiah and King of the Jews to end his earthly reign.

The next time you think, 'How could the Jewish people have missed the fact that Jesus was their Messiah?' put yourself in their position. When they cried out to Jesus on Palm Sunday 'HOSANNAH', they were pleading with him to 'Save/rescue us' from the oppression of Rome.

Yes, we know he ultimately wins in the end. Yes, we know that Yeshua conquered death. Yes, we now know why his ministry looked so different from what the Jewish people were expecting.

But so many didn't recognize the 'why's' back then. Next time you talk about Jesus to someone Jewish, be sure to put yourself 'in their shoes', and speak from a place of love and understanding.

God Loves People
אנשים אוהב אלוהים

God Loves People More Than Anything is a song sung by the group, Point of Grace. We sang the song as a family when our boys were young, and included it in most every Hart Family concert. The words of the chorus, penned by Jon Mohr and John Randall Dennis are simple:

God loves people more than anything
And more than anything,
He wants them to know
He'd rather die than let them go
Cause God loves people more than anything.

Those are simple yet profound words. On the 14th of February, Valentine's Day is recognized and celebrated. Granted, I understand that this is not a Jewish Feast Day or holiday. So why am I writing about it? We're the *Harts*, and with a last name like that, we're almost expected to celebrate love.

I could delve into the history of Valentine's Day, whether it was founded upon the celebration of Lupercalia, or the martyred saint that was named Valentine. But instead, I choose to focus on the love we have received from our Creator and Savior. There is no greater love, no purer love, nor a more sacrificial love than what was shown to us by Jesus, *Yeshua Ha Mashiach*.

From the foundation of the world, sacrifice was part of the fabric of love designed by God Himself. Before the first word of creation was spoken into being by The Word Himself (John 1:1-14), the greatest gift of love was planned out. The very Word of God became human flesh, and loved us all so much, that he gave the ultimate sacrifice.

There never will be a greater gift. Yeshua loved people more than his physical life. He chose to die, in order to save and redeem humankind.

The majority of you have probably heard the above words for years. My prayer for you is that the reality and depth of love displayed by our Creator for us will attach itself to your heart in such a way that you can barely utter your words of thanks to him without experiencing his love in a fresh wave of gratitude.

In 1965, my birth mother went to Sweden to have my life aborted. I should not be here. I should never have been born. I learned this information when I was forty-one years old. For some reason, every abortion clinic during my birth mother's time in Sweden, denied her an abortion. Finding this information out as an adult has changed the way I see life. *What great love* the Father has shown me, by revealing this past event in my life. You spared my life, while I was still in the womb. *Thank you for your love.*

In 2016, you called our youngest son, Ryan, to your Holy Land. This life that I birthed, raised, and loved, you had predestined to live, work, and fulfill his calling in Israel. *Israel*! He is daily helping the Jewish people and living in the city where you died and raised again from the dead. The fact that you chose a man that I made for such an unbelievable purpose for your people amazes and humbles me beyond words. *Thank you for your love.*

Yeshua, you had every right to parade through this earth in your royal robes, while flaunting your strength and majesty. Instead, you chose to walk humbly among commoners. You spoke to men and women in simple terms, while simultaneously explaining truths beyond our imagination and comprehension.

You taught and loved the children. You saw the beauty and value of every life. You took on the sins of every being that had been and every life that would be. Because of you excruciating pain and humiliation, I am now free. *Thank you for your love.*

When thinking about Valentine's Day I can't pass up recognition of the man I am privileged to 'do life' with every single day. Years before I met him, he heard a voice tell him, "Just go ahead and drive off this cliff. It won't matter if you're alive or not." He almost did. Thank you for sparing his life that night. Your grace, mercy, and love are ultimately stronger than any voice that tries to persuade us otherwise. Thank you for orchestrating David's life so that you would breathe life and hope into his soul—and that you brought the two of us together. *Thank you for your love.*

Today please remember: God loves you more than *anything*.

New Insight
חדשה תובנה

So what will this year hold for all of us? What adventures lie within the months ahead for you?

David and I are amazed and so humbled for the path God opened for us with Zola Levitt Presents. We have journeyed to places physically, emotionally, and spiritually that we never dreamed possible.

Some of my greatest personal moments been in Israel. No matter how many times one travels to that land, there is always something new to learn. Each tour brings to light new insights, and revelations. Just when we think we 'know the Bible', God surprises us by revealing '*ah-ha*' moments in our lives. The Bible truly is alive.

May I share an insight from 2017? On our Zola Fall Tour, our tour group visited Tel Megiddo. (A

Tel is an archeological mount/mountain/hill that usually has many layers of previous civilization. Instead of destroying a town or village, those conquering an area would usually build right on top of the ruins—which wondrously preserves ancient history.) Tel Megiddo was an ancient Canaanite city next to the Valley of Armageddon.

Our amazing tour guide (they're fantastic on Zola Tours!) brought us through the Visitor's Center, and was explaining the digs and findings at Tel Megiddo in front of a large replica of the area. As he was pointing out the ancient dwellings and walls, he pointed to the area outside the city walls, and said, "Because there were over 450 horses in ancient Megiddo, people built houses just outside of the walls (to avoid the horse scents!). Any small gathering of houses outside the walls were called 'daughters'. So those houses were the 'daughters of Megiddo'."

He kept teaching the group, but my mind stuck on that 'daughters of Megiddo' phrase. I couldn't get the verse, "Rejoice greatly, O Daughter of Zion" out of my mind. I also couldn't stop singing (in my head, only) the soprano aria written by Handel in his famous work, Messiah, featuring that very verse. I always thought *daughter* meant literal daughters, or decedents. I always envisioned little girls dancing and singing when I heard that phrase.

While some in the group were exiting the replica display room, I politely raised my hand, and asked the tour guide, "Excuse me, but your reference to the daughters of Megiddo...would that also apply to Jerusalem? Would the 'Daughter of Zion' Bible verse also be referring to houses outside of the walls of Zion or Jerusalem?" He answered quickly, "Yes! Exactly."

As we walked around the ancient ruins, my mind 'chewed' on the new information I had just received. *'So if the daughters of Megiddo were houses, then the Daughters of Zion meant houses, too.'* I'm not a deep theologian, but this was pretty simple to reason. Houses, or those people living outside the walls of Zion and Jerusalem were to rejoice. Salvation was available to those 'outside', too.

Rejoice greatly, O daughter of Zion! Shout aloud, O daughter of Jerusalem! Behold, your king is coming to you; righteous and having salvation is he, humble and mounted on a donkey, on a colt, the foal of a donkey. (Zechariah 9:9)

What was simply another verse in the Bible has now given me additional insight into the heart of God. It's the same message that our founder, Zola Levitt shared for decades. Yes, Yeshua was the Messiah for the Jewish people, but we who live 'outside the walls' of Judaism also get to rejoice. He also is *our* King and salvation. Our rejoicing should be (as the verse states) *great*.

In this coming year, may God's living word become alive deep within your soul. May he give you new insight and revelation of his great love for you.

Prodigal Son

האובד הבן

A chapter by David Hart

For some reason, one of my favorite stories in the Bible I am drawn to comes from Luke 15:11 – 32. It is the story of the Prodigal Son. The other day Kirsten and I were discussing the fact that someone we knew who had just received a large inheritance. When my father passed away about ten years ago, my inheritance was a Ziplock baggie full of cheap costume jewelry, cuff links, tie clips, etc. from yard sales and thrift stores. Although I loved my father dearly, there was little if any 'inheritance' whatsoever.

I am a pastor's son. (Yes, we were typically the worst kids from hanging with the deacon's kids.) I'd like to share my thoughts with you on that statement. Because I was a pastor's son, every time the church doors were open, I was there. I was there because I *had* to be there. If I wasn't present, the church people would be sure to let my parents know that I was "missed".

As a young teen, I wanted to fit in with the cool kids. I remember my first Sunday at our new church when I was in junior high. I wore white tube socks and sandals. We had just moved from Southern California to Indiana, and apparently the California styles were vastly different than what everyone was wearing in Indiana at that time. I remember the cute girls snickering at my outfit and it affected me.

I always felt the need to "fit in". Later on in my college days, still feeling the need to be with the "IT" crowd, I made some choices that were not the best. I know now that everything we go through in our lives is a part of our testimony.

So, back to the Prodigal Son. No, I didn't ask for an early inheritance, and no I didn't waste it on wild living, and no I didn't end up sleeping with the pigs. I do, however, remember feeling like the Prodigal must have felt when he decided to go back home to his father. I, too, felt unworthy of anything and would have worked as a servant. I will share one story with you from my rebellion days.

In my mid-twenties, I lived in Los Angeles. Trying to make it in secular music, one night I found myself on top of a lounge bar singing songs about breaking up relationships, and all kinds of depressing themes. My manager at the time, found out I was a preacher's kid and demanded I sing a gospel tune in my bar gig! I was so mad and did not want to be a hypocrite. At one point, I even put my fist thru a wall displaying my refusal to sing gospel.

A lady one night was sitting on a barstool, smoking a clove cigarette. As I was singing, her cigarette smoke was filling my lungs so bad that at that moment, I felt something had to change in my lifestyle.

For two years of my life, I was trying just about anything I could to make it in Hollywood. I remember hearing the Lord speak to me literally every day. My response was, "Lord, when I get that big opportunity, and when an amazing door opens for me, I will give you my full life."

I now know with all of my heart that Yeshua was protecting me from an early death. I am thankful that he is always waiting for us with open arms to come back to him, just as the father was waiting for his prodigal son.

Instead of taking the role of a servant, the father put a robe on his back and a ring on his finger, then threw a huge party welcoming him home. There will always be those like the prodigal's brother who don't understand why their father would be so forgiving.

Who are you the parable? Are the prodigal? A servant? The brother? Are you the rebellious son, lost and far from God? Are you the self-righteous brother, no longer capable of rejoicing when a lost brother finds his way home?

I just finished reading "What About Us" by Eitan Shishkoff. He is on ZLP teaching in our series Called Together. In his chapter, Return of the Lost Son, he compared the Prodigal Son story to Jewish men and women coming back to Yeshua

Ha'Mashiach. What a wonderful comparison for us to know the Father is waiting with open arms for all of his children to return to him. You must read his book.

Possibly you are like I was…almost at rock-bottom. Listening to God, coming to your senses, and deciding to literally run back to God's open arms of compassion and grace and mercy will change your life. If you are hearing his small voice saying, "Return to me, I'm here waiting for you", do it now. Don't wait. Don't talk yourself out of being unworthy of his "welcome home". Now is the time.

If your life has been turned around, we'd love to hear your miracle story. Write to us, and share your "welcome home".

Snooze Ya Lose

מאבד אתה לישון

I don't mean to be disrespectful with this title. But I raised boys. Boy moms are a little more 'real' if you will. So what does the term 'snooze ya lose' have to do with *anything* about Israel? Let me explain.

We've been working on the new series, 'Called Together'. Eitan Shihkoff (Messianic teacher who lives in Israel) brings some great insight and in-depth teaching on the relationships and needed friendships between Jew and Gentile.

Eitan so wonderfully teaches on the Feast of Passover and Shavuot (Feast of Weeks/Pentecost), and how they relate to the life of a gentile Believer. I have learned so much from Eitan's teaching.

As I read, watch, and learn, I feel as if I have missed out on a lifetime of not knowing about the wonderful 'roots' we Christian Believers have. In years of attending church service after church service, I have never been taught the deep significance of the *moadim* (the appointed times). I never even *heard* the word moadim! We're so missing out. As if we've been snoozing through the Old Testament...hence the 'Snooze Ya Lose' title.

Don't get me wrong. I love the churches we've been a part of. I am who I am because of so many believers and teachers in those fellowships. I just feel that by leaving out (at the very least) the knowledge of the Feast Days and appointed times (moadim), that we can't fully understand the complete message that Jesus/Yeshua brought us.

If we aren't teaching about the seven feasts, how can we understand the fact that Yeshua was the fulfillment? If we don't know the symbolism in the Seder, how are we to recognize the symbolism of Holy Communion?

Sure, the grape juice/wine represents the blood spilled for us, and the (usually leavened!) bread represents his broken body. But once you add in the knowledge of how communion comes *from* the Passover meal---then you get the full sense of the symbolism. Since being involved with Zola Levitt Ministries, I feel as if the veil has been lifted, and I'm no longer 'snoozing'!

We have had the wonderful opportunity to devour many of Zola's books in the past months. His books are simultaneously so insightful and deep, while balanced with easy-to-understand common day vernacular. Thank you, Zola Levitt!

His *A Christian Love Story* book was an eye opener. For decades I've heard the verse, "My

Father's house has many rooms; if that were not so, would I have told you that I am going to prepare a place for you?" ((John 14:2 NIV) I simply thought (my whole life!) that this verse meant that Jesus is simply going to prepare a wonderful place for us when we die.

Thanks to Mr. Zola Levitt, my eyes have been opened to what that verse actually means. You can't understand what Jesus is talking about if you don't know the Jewish customs of marriage. (Why isn't this being taught in our churches?) A room was to be built as an addition on to the bridegroom's father's house. The groom would bring his bride to this room.

I'm not going to give the rest of it away. If you don't know what traditionally would happen in a Jewish marriage/wedding, you simply can't understand the significance of John 14:2. (If you haven't already read this book of Zola's, I highly recommend it! It's a fantastic read!)

The purpose of this chapter is not to have Christian pastors upset with me. If you are teaching your congregations the Jewish roots of their faith, I applaud you. I feel that David and I are representative of the majority of Christians sitting in church services every Sunday. We're the 'Everyman' of Evangelical Christianity, if you will.

We're losing out. We have strayed so far away from our Jewish roots, that we can't recognize the Jewishness of our Savior any more. Even 'photos' (really, were cameras around in 30 A.D.?) or paintings of him portray the Savior as a white-skinned, blue-eyed thin Caucasian man. Nine out of ten times, when he is portrayed in a film, he speaks with a thick British accent. We're so far off base.

I am glad that you are reading this book! I am thrilled that you have a hunger and thirst for the truth about the faith we walk in. Yeshua revealed himself through the Old Testament *and* the New Testament. He revealed himself to his chosen people, the Jewish people. He called them apart, to be his witnesses to the world. The more we learn about anything and everything Jewish, the more we learn about the heart of God.

Wherever you are in your journey of learning about your faith, know that everyone is at a different level. Hopefully you also desire to share the message to the Jew first, and also to the Greek. As for me and my household, we are done napping.

Don't get me wrong, I enjoy a good Sunday afternoon 'snooze' as much as anyone. But spiritually? I'm wide awake. I don't want to lose out anymore on not knowing about the beautiful roots planted by Yeshua Ha'Mashiach (Jesus the Messiah) thousands of years ago.

To my Jewish believers in Yeshua, I'm jealous. I'm sure biblically, I shouldn't be, but I am. You truly are the Promised. Will you be patient with us *goyim**? We're learning. Teach us the significance of your Jewish traditions, customs, laws, and way of life. Bake the Harts some *challa*...cause we really like *challa*. Requesting delicious, braided egg bread seems like a good way to end this chapter. And so with that...Shalom.

*goyim is the Jewish name for a non-Jew

A Taste Of Israel

ישראל של טעם

You need to know we love the food of Israel. There I said it. The food of the Holy Land is worth the trip alone. It's life changing. It's one of the reasons we can't wait for each tour. To lead music, worship with all of you, and grow spiritually in God's land...yes. But breakfast, lunch and dinner are highlights of any trip to the Holy Land.

I was raised in New Jersey, and David was raised in Southern California. I'm almost embarrassed to admit that neither of us had eaten hummus prior to our first trip to Israel. I *know*. How did we exist? I've had my fair share of matzo crackers (love them!), fresh *challa*, and matzo ball soup from growing up in the East Coast, but the experience of tasting fresh Israeli cuisine was life changing!

God calls his land the land flowing with milk and honey. In Exodus 33, verse 3, he states, "Go up to the land flowing with milk and honey." (He then proceeds to call his people stiff-necked, but we won't go into that conversation now.)

Deuteronomy 31:20, also mentions milk and honey. Numbers 13:23 tells us the fruit samplings that the Israelites brought to Moses. "When they reached the Valley of Eshkol, they cut off a branch bearing a single cluster of grapes. Two of them carried it on a pole between them, along with some pomegranates and figs." (NIV)

A cluster of grapes, pomegranates and figs doesn't even begin to show what incredible produce this land brings forth. Israel's bounty of wholesome food is a miracle in itself. The majority of the terrain is desert. Dry, barren desert. Yet out of this ground comes some of the greatest food on the planet. I know, because I consumed it daily while I was there. In a world of GMO plants and fruit, the land of Israel brings forth pure, whole vitamin-rich produce unlike anywhere in the world.

Throughout the Jordan River Valley today are orchards after orchards and fertile farmlands producing year-round crops. Dates, bananas, tomatoes, cucumber, and practically every vegetable and fruit is produced in exploding quantities. To most of the world, this is a surprising fact. But God promised this in the Old Testament.

In the book of Ezekiel, it was prophesied, "But you, mountains of Israel, will produce branches and fruit for my people Israel, for they will soon come home. I am concerned for you and will look on you with favor; you will be plowed and sown, and I will cause many people to live on you—yes, all of Israel." Ezekiel 36, 8-10 NIV

Even in its food, Israel is in the middle of fulfilling ancient prophecy. Prophecy coming alive before our very eyes! So exciting! Even more exciting, is that we are able to taste and partake of this prophetic word.

I couldn't wait. My first week home from our last tour to Israel, I *needed* fresh hummus and Israeli salad. Israeli salad is a food that you are blessed to eat for lunch, dinner, *and* breakfast! Yes, salads for breakfast. It's the Israeli way, and it's so healthy.

I ate and ate through our tour, and only gained three pounds over a twenty-day period. That's pretty good, considering I ate my way through the dessert table every night, too! So I needed hummus and Israeli salad.

My hummus wasn't as smooth as what I had just enjoyed in Israel, but I made a pretty good Israeli salad out of tomato, cucumber, onion, garlic, olive oil, parsley, and finally lemon juice. It was so satisfying to have a taste of Israel in my Missouri kitchen.

So what about that milk of the 'milk and honey'? Here's a fun fact about the cows in Israel. They are producers! I mean, honestly, cows in Israel are the best milk producers in the world. Look it up! The facts are there. They're even called 'Super Cows'!

Thousands of years ago, God spoke about the milk! Here we are, with the cows of Israel producing the most milk out of cows across the world. That just makes me smile.

There is so much about the land of Israel that is miraculous. God not only provided a beautiful land for his people, he also provided a land with soil that would produce everything his people needed...and then some. I don't know if we *need* fresh dates, but they are one of the most succulent treats to eat. A date for dessert? Perfect.

If you've never been to Israel to enjoy its cuisine, I encourage you to go! Hopefully in the near future we can share a table together in Israel, and taste of the Lord's bounty!

Traditions
מסורות

Not too long ago, I was chatting with both of our adult sons. We were talking about traditions in our immediate family, and apparently (according to my sons), we really don't have any holiday traditions.

"Yes, we do! We all watch ELF at Christmas time, and The Santa Claus movie", I chimed in. But that was a lame attempt to fill in the realization that I had failed my family to a certain degree. I had lacked forming longstanding family Christmas traditions. Tyler and Ryan, I am sorry.

One year I bought a turkey breast. I thought it would be so much simpler than having to cook a whole turkey plus all of the Christmas meal side dishes out of our tiny oven. Apparently, the turkey breast I bought was actually a lump of non-sliced pressed turkey lunch meat! Saltiest turkey ever. So much for starting a new 'easier' turkey alternative tradition.

I love studying traditions. Particularly traditions that God's people keep. One of my all-time favorite portions of scripture is found in Joshua. When the Israelites finally crossed into the Holy Land, across/through the Jordan River, God spoke to Joshua: "Select twelve men from the people, a man from each tribe, and tell them, 'From right here, the middle of the Jordan where the feet of the priests are standing firm, take twelve stones. Carry them across with you and set them down in the place where you camp tonight.'"

They did as God commanded, and then set up a stone altar on the western bank of the Jordan. "Each of you heft a stone to your shoulder, a stone for each of the tribes of the People of Israel, so you'll have something later to mark the occasion. When your children ask you, 'What are these stones to you?' you'll say, 'The flow of the Jordan was stopped in front of the Chest of the Covenant of God as it crossed the Jordan—stopped in its tracks. These stones are a permanent memorial for the People of Israel.'" (Joshua chapter 4, verses 1-7)

I love that God wanted those that witnessed this miracle to tell their children and the following generations what he did for them. Now that's the kind of tradition I want in my home! A memorial of sorts. A physical reminder of what God has done for us, in the life of our family.

I can just imagine little Israelite children playing in the Jordan, and one asking, "Mom, what's that big pile of rocks for?", and the mother cuddling her child on her lap, and telling the amazing story of how God 'swept away' the mighty waters, and the whole nation of Israel walked across without getting a single drop of water on them. And every time they came to that spot hearing, "Mommy, tell me about those rocks, again, please!"

A tradition, where one verbally recalls God's power and miracles is the kind of tradition worth keeping in your family. Shabbat dinner begins with the lighting of candles to celebrate that God first created light. The blessing of the children comes next. Starting with the oldest, the parents will put their hands on the child's head and give the child a blessing. For both boys and girls, the final part of the blessing is:

May God Bless you and guard you.
May the light of God shine upon you, and may God be gracious to you.
May the presence of God be with you and give you peace.

This beautiful Shabbat blessing is spoken every week. It's a weekly tradition of blessing your children. I'm not trying to make your family tradition of eating Christmas Chex Mix while watching White Christmas sound trivial. God is the one who instilled a love of traditions in us. I just think we need to balance out the fun/trivial 'we do this every year' with some 'what God has done in our lives' symbolic activities.

Perhaps there are certain Christmas tree ornaments that remind you of times when God has interceded, or blessed you. I have seen 'Our First Year' or 'Baby's First Christmas' ornaments. When you hang those particular ornaments, take a few moments to verbally remember how God worked to bring the two of you together.

Share with your child as he or she gets older, what a miracle it was to have them come into your life. What a blessing, as you hang those 'first year' ornaments, to share with your family times of blessings and remembrances.

Psalm 34 verse 8 tells us to "Taste and see that the LORD is good; blessed is the one who takes refuge in him." This scripture is a wonderful reminder in s season when we tend to gorge ourselves on turkey, stuffing, green bean casserole, pies, and candies. In the midst of the seasonal partying, eating, and festivities, it is because of the Lord's goodness in our lives that we are able to feast, and enjoy special times with our loved ones.

You may be reading this book in the middle of the summer, but it's never too early to plan and prepare for coming seasons. This *next* Christmas and Hanukkah season, may you indeed 'Taste and see that the Lord is good'.

As you keep old traditions passed down from generation to generation, and instill new ones, may they be beautiful reminders of God's goodness and faithfulness.

Jerusalem's Cats
בירושלים החתולים

Yes it's the Holy Land. Yes, we walk in the footsteps of Yeshua. Yes, the Bible comes alive when we journey to Israel. But can I be honest with you? One of the things I love about being in Jerusalem is the cats!

The holiest city on earth is also inhabited by over two million *cats*. Now if you're not an animal lover, you'll need to be patient with me through this chapter. I'll tie it into a spiritual point, no worries. But if you love cats, you'll appreciate where I'm taking all of this.

Our first time to Jerusalem, no one told us about the cat population. We were walking through the Old City, and noticing these adorable cats perching themselves on ancient walls, as if not a care in the world.

Short hair, long hair, calico, seal-pointed, grey and white striped tabbies all strut through the rugged stone and brick pathways. History tells us that when the British began their 'rule' over Jerusalem, they brought cats in to ward off the rat population. Since then, the cats have established themselves as the dominant street residents.

The last time we were at The Western Wall (*Ha Kotel*), I noticed an orange and white tabby sauntering to a 'sun spot'. There it casually reclined and started grooming itself. In the midst of thousands of humans that made their once-in-a-lifetime pilgrimage to this very holy spot, here's this cat just casually grooming its fur.

Of course I went up to it to say, "Hi!" Then it hit me (a thought, not the cat...). Do these cats only understand Hebrew? How should I greet a Jerusalem cat? Is "Here kitty, kitty" a phrase it would understand? Is the word "Shalom" understood by street cats? Did this striped feline understand that it *lived* where so many humans from across the world can only dream of going?

Not to worry. The fact that Judah's capital is filled with *felines* hasn't passed me by. Judah, the ancient Southern Kingdom's capitol was Jerusalem. And their symbol? The *Lion* of Judah.

Here we are, thousands of years later with 'mini' Lion of Judah's (if you will), reminding us of the original and rightful heirs of this city. And yes, our Lord himself is described as the Lion of Judah.

When Jacob (*Israel*) referred to his son Judah as 'Young Lion', I wonder if he had *any* idea that miniature relatives of the lion family would inhabit that same land today.

> *"You, Judah, your brothers will praise you:*
> *Your fingers on your enemies' throat,*
> *while your brothers honor you.*
> *You're a lion's cub, Judah,*
> *home fresh from the kill, my son.*
> *Look at him, crouched like a lion, king of beasts;*
> *who dares mess with him?"*
> (Genesis 49:8-9 NIV)

Honestly, I'm a tad jealous of these cats. Jerusalem is their home. Do they *get* that where they live is the ultimate destination for believers in Yeshua? Do they know the significance of the streets they roam? Do they understand that Yeshua was *raised from the dead* and healed all that came to him right where they live everyday life?

Just as I'm sure that the cats of Jerusalem don't 'get' the significance of where they live, many of us humans don't get the significance of *who* we are. The Lion of Judah Himself abides within us. We are filled with that same power. Yet we walk around, as the cats in Jerusalem, unaware of the power within our reach.

> *"Now to him who is able to do immeasurably more*
> *than all we ask or imagine, according to his*
> *power that is at work within us, to him be glory in*
> *the church and in Christ Jesus throughout all*
> *generations, for ever and ever! Amen."*
> (Ephesians 3:20-21)

We have the Holy Spirit's power available 24/7 in our lives. The resurrection power that was displayed over 2000 years ago in *Yerushalayim* is available to us right now. Unfortunately, too often we end up being the orange tabby at the Western Wall. We sit clueless of what's within our reach, and simply go about life's daily routines as usual.

Next time you're in Jerusalem, take notice of the street kitties. They're subtle reminders of the Lion of Judah that will soon be reigning from that unbelievable city for 1,000 years. The Lion of Judah will once again roar with power and reign with strength.

"And one of the elders said to me, 'Stop weeping; behold, the Lion that is from the tribe of Judah, the Root of David, has overcome so as to open the book and its seven seals.'"
(Revelation 5:5)

This sweet cat lives near the Upper Room! Can't

resist a little 'street cat loving'.

Do you notice the famous gold-domed Dome of the
Rock in the upper right part of the photo?

God's Moadim

ימים מינה אלוהים

Three Moadim, or Feasts take place in the Fall.
Before starting my position as the Co-Host for Zola
Levitt Presents, I honestly had never heard the word
moadim. But now it's a word that has deep
meaning. In 2018, all of the three fall feasts occured
in September (that doesn't always happen). These
are special months to celebrate days that God
Himself set aside for us to observe.

In Leviticus, God announced his appointed
times, *moadim.* They were days that all of Israel
were to observe. Four times in the spring, and three
in the fall. Our television ministry's founder, Zola
Levitt, wrote a wonderful (and easy to read) book
explaining the significance of these feasts titled The
Seven Feasts of Israel.

If you haven't read the book, I highly suggest

that you do. The significance of the feasts for the Jewish people, and we who believe in Yeshua, are beautifully explained in only a way Zola could script.

I am sure that there are others (including Zola) that could explain and teach the feast days to you far better than I could ever do. I won't even attempt a 'teach' but rather simply 'share' from my heart.

As tour leaders, we pray that every person on our tour will have an 'I know *that I know* God met me there' location or moment in time. I like to think of it as having a 'personal moadim'.

People may think, "Why go to Israel?" God can meet you anywhere you are. That is true. But if you've been, you know that there is an anointing on that very land. There just is. One of those anointed spots we visit is Shiloh, the site of the first Tabernacle. I, first hand, was able to witness one of the women on our tour experience her personal moadim.

On the day we visited ancient Shiloh, it was just an 'ordinary' day. It wasn't a set appointed biblical feast day that God mentioned in the book of Leviticus. Yet next to the very spot where the Holy of Holies (the inner chamber of the Tabernacle) stood for 369 years, our pilgrim (we'll call her Abebi) took of her sandals and called down the Spirit of God. I believe God himself met with her that day.

We had all experienced the phenomenal movie about Shiloh as we sat up in the theater overlooking the ancient Tabernacle site. It's a highlight of our whole tour. When we all left the theater, we (as a group) walked down the hill and sat in a spot that was the outer court of the tent.

A holy hush fell on the group as we sat in awe of the land we were sitting on. We shared some verses about the Tabernacle, and then had the opportunity to have some 'alone time' if we so desired before all meeting back on the bus.

I slowly walked and prayed around the archeological digs of the ancient tent. As most of our people were making their way back to the bus, I noticed Abebi. Abebi was from Nigeria, and she was one of my favorites. There were still a few of us down at the Tabernacle site praying, and having our quiet times. Abebi wasn't so quiet.

Beside where Abebi was calling to God were her sandals. They were off. She knew she was standing on holy ground. Abebi prayed and called out with a fervor from deep within her soul. She was simultaneously praising God, and requesting of him (like Hannah did at that very spot thousands of years ago) for her needs and the needs of her loved ones. The Bible is full of verses of those who cried out to God. Abebi was doing the same.

"In my distress I called to the LORD; I cried to my God for help. From his temple he heard my voice; my cry came before him, into his ears." Psalm 118:6 (NIV)

She, David, and I were the last of our tour at the site. It was time to get back to the bus, but I knew she was having a divine appointment with the God of Israel. We waited a bit longer. When God is meeting with someone, it's hard to tell them, "You need to get on the bus, because we have lunch reservations at a restaurant." But God had met with her, and she started walking towards the entrance to the site with us.

God's appointed times, his moadim, are set for the Jewish people. Yet through His Holy Spirit, the God of Israel desires to meet with *you*. Be ready. And if you decide to journey to Israel with us, come expectant of times of meeting with the Holy one.

This is the same spot where Abebi was calling out to God. These rocks were next to the Tabernacle at Shiloh. The Holy of Holies spot for hundreds of years, and the spot where the twelve tribes of Israel would gather for the Feasts.

Everyday Savior
היומיומי המושיע

Have you ever been around someone that spoke on such a deep intellectual level that you left the conversation thinking that you function at such a mediocre capacity? Feeling as if you don't have the vocabulary or insight to communicate with someone else can make you feel extremely inadequate. If you ever played the game Trivial Pursuit with a science or history major, and answered a question wrong, you know the feeling.

The good news? You have a savior that never talked down to people, or made anyone feel that they couldn't grasp 'Kingdom' insights. I learned this truth walking the Holy Land.

I attended Sunday school every single week of my life growing up (except for the few and rare sick days). I even attended Bible College. But it wasn't until I walked the rocky and dusty roads of the Galilee in Israel that I fully comprehend that God Himself, while being infinitely beyond human understanding, has the compassionate ability to communicate on a level every human can relate to.

While touring the Mount of Beatitudes, I noticed gorgeous yellow flowers sprawled throughout the mountainside. I asked our tour guide what those flowers were, and he stated, "Those are wild mustard plants. They grow rampant in this region." I could envision wild mustard plants right where the crowds would have been sitting when our Savior was teaching them about the Kingdom of God.

Although the Sermon on the Mount comes before Yeshua's teaching about the mustard seed (which is found in Matthew 13), the teaching was all in the same area. If you've been there, you know the Beatitude's teaching and the parables of Matthew 13 literally took place just yards away from each other.

In both instances, the hillside was full of farmers, and people that worked the fields on a daily basis. Agriculture was what the Galileans knew. We in modern-day America, don't experience wild mustard plants growing in our yards. The shrub is native to Africa, India and the Middle East. So when we read a parable about a mustard seed, it is something foreign to us. Special, different, beautiful, but not common and every day.

While we perhaps envision a parable about faith and a mustard seed being 'deep' and insightful, the Galileans understood what Jesus was teaching from a different viewpoint.

As their children sat on the ground, listening to this teacher from Nazareth, I envision the little ones rolling mustard seeds between their fingers, and perhaps counting the individual seeds in a bloom. Only the Creator of all could be so brilliant to teach of his Kingdom using the natural beauty and elements that he himself spoke into being.

Yeshua knew this land. It was his neighborhood. He knew how his people thought. He understood that humans learn better when a topic is related to through on a common everyday occurrence. Walking the fields adorned with wild mustard seed bushes, while at the same time relating these wild growing plants to the faith one might have is pure brilliance.

How often do we sit and think about how tiny our faith can be in order to move whatever mountain we may be facing? Your Savior knows your thoughts. I believe, through his teachings on a tiny, common seed, we can know that nothing is impossible with God. Just as Christ desired to teach the Jewish people thousands of years ago attainable Kingdom knowledge, I believe he wants all of us to know those truths.

In these photos I took in Israel, notice the vast amount of yellow flowered mustard. And to think...all of that started with one tiny seed. Let your faith grow today.

Wild mustard bushes growing in Northern Israel.
This is the area of ancient Tel Dan, and the
mountains in the distance are Lebanon!

Sounds of Silence
שתיקה של קולות

If you are a church goer, you have probably sung the song Silent Night many times in your life. It's a beautiful Christmas Carol, and one we often sing on Zola Tours when we are in Bethlehem. What is so beautifully contradictory, is that birthing a baby in a stable with animals possibly present isn't the quietest scene.

I didn't grow up on a farm, but I've spent enough time around farm animals to know that they're a noisy bunch. And unless Mary was the world's quietest woman, birthing can be an event filled with sounds of pain. Combine the 'manger scene' with that of a vast host of angels loudly proclaiming *'Glory to God in the highest, and on earth peace, good will towards men'* across the sky, I'd say it was probably a rather boisterous event.

I am a woman that appreciates the reverence of a subdued worship experience. I attended an all-girl's Catholic school for eighth grade. I respected the piety of silence and stillness. I just don't think our Creator is a silent type.

In the beginning, we are told that God spoke into being every single planet, star, and galaxy. Somehow I can't envision the Word of God whispering a galaxy into being. I also can't comprehend that a sky full of angels would softly speak the greatest news ever given to mankind. The *Savior was born*! The time of salvation for mankind had come! *Glory to God*!

True, we know from reading I Kings chapter 19 that God spoke to Elijah in a 'still small voice', but that isn't His customary voicing. Even in the so-called 'silent years' between the Old and New Testaments, God was definitely speaking. Perhaps he wasn't speaking through a major prophet, but he was speaking to those who would listen and obey. We know that truth because of the events that happened with the Maccabean revolt.

It was always interesting to me that God could be silent for over 400 years. His nature isn't to be quiet, yet Bible teachers almost portray God as 'sitting on his hands with tape over his mouth' during that period. That's because the Evangelical Christian church doesn't teach us about the miracles surrounding the Feast of Lights.

Judah Maccabee, a Jewish priest, led a revolt against the Seleucid Empire that was horrifically desecrating the Temple. Judah reclaimed the Temple, and re-consecrated it. I'm sure if you have followed Zola Levitt, you know the rest of this story. God spoke to Judah Maccabee and his followers. God was speaking to those who listened to Him. Those assumed 'silent years' were full of activity.

Whether you observe Hanukkah, Christmas (or both!), may you find peace in the midst of the business of that season. The angels proclaimed (with a mighty and strong voice, I believe) to the shepherds in Bethlehem thousands of years ago a message of *good news*.

May God continue to speak words of life, encouragement, and inspiration into your family. He *may* do it with a still small voice, but don't be surprised if God boisterously wants to exclaim his power and messages of hope.

Rimonim

רימון

Every year on our Zola Fall Tour, we visit Greece (which by the way is quite spectacular). Nanda is our Greek tour guide, and she is simply the best. On the day that our tour visits the city (ruins) of Ancient Corinth, we have the opportunity to drive our very large tour bus through the delightful, quaint, charming, and *narrow* streets of 'modern day' (although it's quite ancient in its own right) Corinth.

One of my favorite things from the height of the tour bus window is to observe as much 'real' everyday life as possible. As we were driving those picturesque streets of Corinth, I was 'oooh-ing and aww-ing' at all the colorful and endearing courtyards filled with vibrant bougainvillea, roses, and flora of the area. The lovely private courtyards ooze of Greek charm. As people on our tours often do, someone asked Nanda, "What is that tree to the left?"

"That's a pomegranate tree! We love them in Greece!" Nanda continued on about the importance of pomegranates on New Year's Day. We were told that Greek families, just after midnight on New Year's Eve, will smash a pomegranate on the floor near their front door! The more seeds that they see, the better luck they'll have that year.

There were a few gasps from the women on the bus. "*But that would stain the floor!*" was the resounding comment. "We just cover that spot up with an area rug. It's a very Greek thing to do." (We love Nanda and her answers.)

I thought it would be fun to let you know how Greeks celebrate bringing in the New Year with one of the Holy Land's seven species. Thought you also might enjoy learning about this amazing fruit that grows abundantly throughout the Holy Land.

In Deuteronomy 8:8, the seven species are listed. These were staple food items that God promised would be found in the Promised Land. They are barley, wheat, grapes, figs, olives, dates, and *pomegranates*. If you've been to Israel, you have probably at least sampled the seven species. If you haven't been to Israel yet, we can arrange that for you!

Throughout the streets of Jerusalem (and at other great spots across Israel), you will find fresh pomegranate juice stands. They will literally 'squeeze/squish' pomegranates until there is enough for you to have a big cup full of the delicious and extraordinarily healthy juice.

In Israel, as in Greece, pomegranates symbolize the New Year. On Rosh Hashanah (not in January), pomegranates are consumed, as well as used as decoration throughout the New Year celebration. An interesting fact that I learned this past tour was that King Solomon's crown was actually fashioned after the 'crown' of the top of a pomegranate!

Now for one of my favorite 'ah-ha' pomegranate insights. One of our Israeli tour guides, Ilan (who is quite famous for his funny jokes), told us that there are supposedly 613 seeds in an individual pomegranate, which parallels the amount of commandments given in the Old Testament. The more I learn about God and His land, the more I fall in love with the detail of God's creation, and how He incorporates such intricacies into His word.

When the twelve spies (in Exodus) went in to the Promised Land to 'scout' it out, they came back with pomegranates to show that the land was literally *fruit*ful. It's just one fruit out of so many that God created, yet he himself chose this ruby red food to symbolize so much, and to be a product that feeds and nourishes his people—even in modern-day Israel.

On our last day in Jerusalem, we all visit the Garden Tomb. It is a beautiful, lush garden spot in the middle of a busy city. As we were preparing the spot where our group would share communion, I noticed a pomegranate tree. I had to capture the beauty that was before my eyes. The deep red open pomegranate was showing off its luscious berries, and its orange shaded 'partner' was proudly displaying its King Solomon crown.

On New Year's Eve, have no worries. We're not expecting you to smash a pomegranate on your floor. But I would like you to remember that the God who can make the seeds of a fruit remind people of his commandments, intricately knows and fashioned *you*. As special as this fruit is to the Holy Land, you are worth far more.

*The Hebrew word for pomegranate is rimonim.

Pomegranates on a pomegranate tree at the Garden
Tomb in Jerusalem.

He'll Make A Way
דרך יעשה הוא

One of the highlights of any tour to the Holy Land is our time at the Western Wall (*Ha Kotel* in Hebrew). If you know anything about Israel, you know that this is *the* site to see. It is the most accessible spot for Jewish to people to pray that physically gets them closest to where the Holy of Holies (in the Temple) was.

Every day you will see hundreds (sometimes thousands) of people praying and worshiping in their own unique way. Orthodox Jews will be saying their prayers, as Christian men and women worship and pray alongside in a beautiful picture of faith in the one and only God of Abraham, Isaac, and Jacob.

Speaking of Abraham and Isaac, Mt. Moriah (the Temple Mount) is also the location where God told

Abraham to offer Isaac as a sacrifice, thousands of years ago. In a world that considered child sacrifice common, and in many ways necessary for pleasing the gods, God requested Abraham to kill his promised son. Abraham was the very first Hebrew, and there weren't any laws or 'traditions' in place yet.

Abraham didn't know what God would require of those who followed him. I can't even imagine what went through Abraham's head and heart when in Genesis 22:2, when God called out to Abraham, "Take your son, your only son, whom you love— Isaac—and go to the region of Moriah. Sacrifice him there as a burnt offering on a mountain I will show you."

Now it's interesting to me that God says 'your only son', even though Abraham had fathered Ishmael, but that discussion is for another time. What in the world was going through Abraham's mind? I would have been thoroughly depressed and utterly confused. And I'll be honest, I would have been *mad*. Really, really mad.

It's a good thing Abraham believed in God *so much* that he knew somehow and someway, he would return from the mountain *with* Isaac. The whole way up the mountain I would have been grumbling, "so much for the whole Father of Nations deal…" (and probably some other not-so-nice words). What kind of conversation with your son *could* you have?

We all know the story. Isaac was literally bound and laying on the altar. (What were his words of explanation for doing *that*??) Abraham, knife in air, ready to plunge it into his beloved child, hears the voice of an angel calling to him. God *did* provide a ram for the sacrifice. Abraham saw a ram, caught in a thicket. Once again, God made a way when there seemed to be no way out.

Every person that visits the Western Wall has a different 'take-away'. Some have placed a tightly rolled prayer into a crevice between the ancient stones. Some have shed tears of sorrow or tears of joy. What do I personally experience? The reminder that God always makes a way for us, even though we can't understand, or don't see a way out.

It's not hard to be reminded of that promise. Know why? The miracles of God are blatantly evident as one looks at the Western Wall. For out of those stones (no dirt around) grow thicket bushes. Yes, thickets—just like the one that caught a ram for Abraham's sacrifice. Just one of the myriad of reminders that Israel is indeed a *holy* land. The God of the Universe wants us to know that he can do the same for us today.

Jehovah Jireh (our Provider) beckons (I believe) birds to somehow carry 'thicket bush seeds' in their tiny feet, so that miraculously these bushes can grow out of rocks, and be a constant visual reminder of his unending faithfulness. How awesome is it for God to provide a living picture of provision on an ancient stone wall.

If God can provide a way for Abraham and Isaac, he can do the same for you today. On that same mountain, God didn't provide a 'scapegoat' for his one and only son. Yehsua was bound, and sacrificed in order that you can be redeemed and set free.

Whatever you're facing—God can 'make a way' when there seems to be no way. Even if you're *that close* to giving up, he can call out to you (even if it's in the last millisecond) and open a door you never thought possible. Abraham trusted God in the midst of a devastingly horrific future. He can do that for you, too. But you must trust him.

David praying at the Western Wall.

Believe-It-Or-Lot

או תאמינו לוט

There are many things in life that challenge us to believe it…or not believe it. When I was a child, I always enjoyed visiting the Ripley's Believe-It-Or-Not museums, and reading through their books. There are some things in books and museums which are simply too big, too odd, or too ridiculous to think true.

The Bible is full of stories and incidences that make its reader question if these stories really could have happened. Six-fingered giants roaming the earth? The sun standing still and not 'moving' for Joshua's battle. How did that happen? Was it an eclipse of some sort? There are many mysteries that we may never know the exact details of until we sit down in Heaven for some chats about these stories.

David and I had been to Israel prior to our tour

hosting with Zola Tours, but we had never before ventured south of Masada. The 'Petra extension' of our tour will take you through exotic ancient Biblical sites. We were on our wonderful tour bus, driving south when our bus driver David said, "And there's Lot's wife to the right." Lot's *wife*? I looked out of the expansive front window of our Immanuel Tour bus and viewed something I never thought possible.

There, before my very eyes was a rock/salt formation that unbelievably looked *exactly* like a woman looking off into the distance behind her. Sure, I've heard of Lot's wife in various sermons and Sunday school lessons throughout my life...but this was different. Before my eyes wasn't a sermon on paper, it was a ginormous physical evidence of a Bible 'story' from the beginning of time. The story of Sodom & Gomorrah, Lot, his wife, daughters, and the angel visitors goes all the way back to Genesis chapter 19. It's difficult to get more 'ancient' than Genesis.

If you know the story, you will recall that two angels came to Lot, and told him to take his wife, daughters, and sons-in-law out of the city, and to flee, because imminent destruction was coming. Lot ended up fleeing with his wife and two daughters only. As the Genesis story states, after they had fled, Lot's wife disobeyed the commands of the angels, and when she looked back to see the destruction, she turned into a pillar of salt.

There are a few more bizarre verses about Lot's daughters, but Lot's wife apparently, literally was *turned into salt*.

Our tour bus stopped, and we were told that we could disembark to take pictures. I needed a few moments to soak it all in. Up on the mountain in front of me was a statue/figure that looked like a giant version of a woman wearing a white head covering/shawl, with a blue full-length robe. Granted, it was a much taller version of a typical woman's body, but it unmistakably looked like a woman frozen in time.

David, our bus driver took a group of us over to the mountain itself, and taught us that all the other mountains in the area were limestone, but this was the only single 100% salt mountain in the whole region (that was literally across the valley of ancient Sodom and Gomorrah). If all the present dirt and sand on the mountain were washed off, we could see a shining pure salt *mountain*.

I took my photos, and a tiny piece of salt-rock (we were given permission), and thought about that majestic 'sculpture' for days. I have the photo you see here, framed, and in my bathroom. You can take the validity of this salt monument with a grain of salt (pun intended), or you can believe that this is the literal preserved woman-turned-salt that we are told about in the book of Genesis.

Either it 100% really *is Lot's wife*, or perhaps people in ancient times *saw* this sculpture of what looks like a woman, and associated it with the 'tale of Lot'? If people simply saw this sculpture, what else could they have 'seen' in Israel, and formed a story/tale about it, or associated it with a Biblical story? The fact that this is the *only salt mountain* in the area is either an interesting coincidence—or it's

Biblical truth coming alive before our very eyes.

My question to you today? Do you Believe-It-Or-Not? Interesting story based on a woman-looking salt figure, or modern-day proof that an ancient story is literal and not just a literary tale?

My chunk of 'Lot's Wife Mountain' salt. It's still unbelievable to hold this in my hand. Under the sand/dirt, you can see the salt crystals.

As The Deer

הצבי כמו

I love writing about our tours to Israel, because every single time we go, we learn hidden insight gems we never knew before. I believe that happens because it truly is God's holy land. God's word *and* land is never stagnant. It's alive and brimming with new wisdom and truths---but we have to 'ready ourselves' to hear and experience it.

David and I grew up in the church, and we were both heavily involved in its music (although we grew up on opposite coasts). Our knowledge and history of church music is one of the things that drew us together when we were first interested in each other.

At camps, in youth groups, and on Sunday mornings, we sang the song *As the Deer* written in 1984 by Martin J. Nystrom. Of course, the *lyrics* were penned by King David thousands of years ago. The worship song version, though, made its way into churches in the 80's.

We've sung the song for years, and I personally always imagined a Bambi-like deer going to drink from a stream in a lush wooded forest glade. That was just the image my mind concocted. I had no idea (even though I have read my Bible since I began to figure out how letters formed words) that the factual deer of Psalm 42 don't look like Bambi...and they don't live in a lush forest.

Ein Gedi is a stop we make on our Petra extension on Zola Tours. It is the desert site where David (before becoming King) hid from Saul in caves situated in this natural reserve. Ein Gedi literally means 'place of the spring goat'. Spring in this sense, does not mean a time of year, rather a fresh water spring. There are mountain goats are called Ibex, that are the 'deer' that David writes about in his psalm. (I think there were was something lost in translation down the line.)

Why write an article about the Ibex at Ein Gedi? Because these 'deer' weren't in a rich, dense forest. Ibex live in the desert. Why did David mention them in his Psalm? Because every day as he was in seclusion, hiding from someone who was threatening to kill him, David saw Ibex come down from the surrounding cliffs and mountains to drink from the steady (miraculous) supply of fresh water in the middle of a dry barren desert. In the cool of the mornings, Ibex can be found (even today!) drinking from the steady supply of water.

David saw these Ibex daily. He knew their eating

and drinking patterns. As the beautiful Ibex longed for their morning drink, so David's soul longed for God. David's *soul* was thirsty to be revived daily by his creator.

If you go with us to Israel, you'll more than likely see Ibex for yourself. They're honestly really cute, and even like to climb in trees! You can catch a glimpse of what David's life was like when he hid in the caves of Ein Gedi. You will see for yourself the barrenness of that wilderness, contrasted with a hidden tropical oasis full of lush vegetation and a constant supply of much needed water tucked into the rough landscape.

Just as these Ibex longed for their daily supply of water, may you continually thirst for truth, righteousness, and for the presence of the Almighty. God was (and *still is*) faithful to supply drinking needs for these Ibex. If he is able to supply for the needs of these animals, know that he desires to take care of *your* needs. Even if on the outside, your life looks barren and desolate…there is a fountain ready to quench your thirst. Enjoy that truth today.

A beautiful and strong Ibex of Ein Gedi.

DAVID & KIRSTEN HART

Life In Israel
בישראל החיים

I took the opportunity to have our youngest son, Ryan answer some questions about life in Israel. He has been living there for three years, and I thought it would be interesting for you to hear what it is like for an American Christian to live in a predominantly Jewish country. Here's what Ryan had to say

1.) What misconceptions do you believe Americans have about Israel?

In my time, I've heard quite a few thoughts on what Israel is like. Many of them saying that Israel is dangerous, which I have found to be the exact opposite. There is also the common idea that Israel is a third world country, and while some areas are not as advanced as others, the central hubs are quite alive and flourishing. Israel is also a pioneer in high tech and medical industries!

2.) What is your biggest struggle (if any) moving to a foreign land?

One of the biggest struggles of moving to a foreign country is trying to buy all of the ingredients you need for cooking! There have been a few times where I will go to the store to buy milk and cereal, only to return home with cereal and yogurt! While it's not the worst combination in the world, it's definitely a shock! But it does make eating at home a bit more difficult, for sure.

3.) What advice would you give an American that wants to move to Israel?

My advice to Americans wanting to move to Israel is to really see if it is God calling you to move to Israel, or just your personal desire to move. I have seen people moving to Israel of their own accord and they have a very difficult time finding their place with everything, however, if it is God calling you, there will be an abundance of open doors.

4.) What would people be surprised to know about

life in Jerusalem?

Something that I think people would be surprised to know about life in Jerusalem is how much nature there is. If you drive ten minutes West out of the city, you have the Jerusalem forest. You drive to the East, you have the Dead Sea and an abundance of mountainous hikes. There is so much life in and around the city that it is hard to be bored!

5.) Do you feel racial/religious tension with the Arabs? Or Jewish people?

There are definitely times where you can feel tensions, but there are many more times where you see friendships pushing through. I will put it this way. If you look for the hatred and animosity, that is what you will find. If you look for the compassion and love, that is what awaits you.

6.) Do you feel safe living in Jerusalem?

I have lived in Jerusalem for two years. In those two years, I have not once felt like I was in danger. There have been times where I got lost in the city, but even then, people were more than willing to help me find my way around, even though we didn't speak the same language. Jerusalem is a city where hundreds of people groups come to visit, and the people of Jerusalem are very kind to everyone!

7.) Where do you buy food/groceries?

Just up the road from where I live is a nice grocery store that has most everything I would need. Across the street from my apartment, there is a gas station that is open on Shabbat so I can pick up any last minute snacks I might want after the Sabbath begins!

If I'm having a lot of people over, I will walk about 30 minutes to go to a store called Rami Levi, which is basically the Israeli Wal-Mart! They have an enormous selection for pretty cheap prices!

8.) What is a 'must-see' location that most tourists don't normally go to see?

A must see location that tours generally don't go is the Mechane Yehuda Shuk. It's an open market where you can buy all kinds of spices, nuts, fruits, vegetables, meats, sweets... basically whatever you want to find, you can probably find it at the Shuk. There are all kinds of hidden alleyways that open up to fantastic restaurants, and the night life there is a blast!

9.) What are the 'must-know' Hebrew words/phrases in order to communicate/live there?

Shalom (hello),
beseder (okay/fine)

slicha (sorry/ excuse me)
laffa falafel bevakasha (falafel in a laffa bread,
please!)

10.) What is the greatest challenge of living in
Israel?

For me, a big challenge of living in Israel is when
good friends move away. Jerusalem is a very
transient city. There are people from all around the
world moving there for anywhere between two
weeks, to twenty years, but it sometimes feels like
just when you've gotten to know someone, they
move away. Thankfully there are always more
people coming to the city though!

11.) What's your favorite Israeli food/meal?

One of my favorite meals in Jerusalem is Melauach!
It's a Yemenite food served at Jachnun Bars, which
are found around Jerusalem as well as around Israel.
It's a light, flaky pastry with hummus, spicy spread,
cheese, tomatoes, olives, onions, fried eggplant,
cauliflower, grilled mushrooms, and sometimes
shakshuka on top! It's cheap, fast, and absolutely
delicious!

12.) What is the greatest attribute Jewish Israeli's
possess?

The Jewish Israelis have a strong sense of self-worth. They know what their time is worth and they want to make the most of it. It's something that is a good message for Americans to have as well. You are important, and you are worth a lot!

13.) The biggest difference between Israelis and Americans?

The language is a big thing, for sure. As well, where Americans can be closed off to people, Israelis are generally very welcoming and treat you like family very quickly.

14.) What do you do on a daily basis with your position   at   the   embassy?

I volunteer at the International Christian Embassy Jerusalem as a Video Production Specialist. That means I help write the scripts, I shoot the videos, I edit them, and do a lot of other roles within the organization as well! I lead worship at our morning devotions, and help wherever I'm needed.

TV taping a song for Zola Levitt Presents with Ryan on The Ramparts, which is an upper walkway on the inner side of the Old City of Jerusalem walls!

You Won't Know Unless You Go!

הולך אתה אם יודע לא אתה

No matter how many times one goes to the Holy Land, there are *always* brand new insights to be discovered. If you haven't had the opportunity to take this journey of a lifetime, I encourage you to take the leap of faith, and sign up for one of our tours. Why? Because if you are physically able, you don't want to miss out on seeing God's beloved land with your own eyes. If you can't go with us on a Zola tour, at least try to find some group that you can go with.

Only a few weeks after one of our tours, I chatted with one of our 'pilgrims' that made the journey. She told me, "I've only been back a few weeks, and I'm ready to go again! I still have so much to learn, and I can't wait to go back to that amazing place."

My favorite part about a Holy Land trip (other than the amazing food, obviously) is the fact that I *learn so much*. I've literally read the Bible my whole life, and yet there are constantly new discoveries that I learn with every trip. I mean *unbelievable* insights I've never been taught before.

I've sat through college Bible courses and attended Bible studies for years. Yet in ten days of touring Israel, my eyes and ears can barely soak in all the new information. What information you ask? Well, I'm going to quickly tell you three of my favorite Israeli trip discoveries. Trust me, there are more, and it's hard to narrow it down to three, but I will give it my best try.

The Acacia Tree

Most of us know that the Ark of the Covenant was formed from acacia wood. What most of us aren't taught is that (in all probability, and as Jewish tradition tells us) the burning bush that God spoke from to Moses was an acacia tree! In the barren wilderness, there isn't much vegetation, but what you *do* see are small acacia trees scattered across the landscape.

God speaking to Moses from the same tree/bush as the Ark of the Covenant (where his earthly presence lived)? Coincidence? Fascinating fact!

Gates of Hell

In Matthew 16:18, Yeshua tells Peter, "And I tell you, you are Peter, and on this rock I will build my church, and the gates of hell shall not prevail against it." Why is this interesting? Because there is a literal spot in Israel called *The Gates of Hell.*

Caesarea Philippi, the ancient city in northern Israel is the location of the headwaters of the Jordan River, but also a cliff where pagans would sacrifice their children (literally throw them off the cliff), and engage in corrupt sexual immorality.

Worship of Ba'al and Pan occurred at this very site. It was believed that an entrance to the underworld was at this very spot. So when Jesus stated, "the gates of hell…" He and his disciples were literally sitting, *looking at the spot* called The Gates of Hell.

Stone Masonry/Carpenter

I've always imagined Jesus' first thirty years of life as a man building tables, kitchen cabinets, and whittling wood. What I didn't imagine was that carpentry in Israel is actually stone masonry!

Houses throughout the Holy Land are made from a pale limestone, also known as Jerusalem stone. Houses 2000 years ago were also made out of limestone, as trees weren't a prevalent natural resource. Even tables, beds, and household 'furniture' items were fashioned out of stone.

There were a few items made out of wood, but it wasn't a common commodity. Those paintings of a frail looking Jesus? Our Savior 'hefted' large stones on a daily basis. Yeshua wasn't frail at all! Stone masons were tough, strong people!

(I am going to give you a quick fourth *bonus* insight!)

Pomegranates are one of the seven species/*Shivat Haminim* (agricultural products) mentioned in Deuteronomy 8:8 that are special products of the Holy Land. You've already read a bit about them in a previous chapter.

Jewish tradition teaches us that the pomegranate is said to have 613 seeds, which corresponds with the 613 *mitzvot*, or commandments, of the Torah. There are so many more fascinating details about pomegranates, but I'd make this chapter way too long!

These are just a few of my favorite personal insights from our trips to the Holy Land. There are so many more. If you have been waiting for a 'sign' that you should go to Israel, well, consider this chapter your sign!

Israel's Golden Anniversary
לישראל הזהב השנה יום

June 2017 was an exciting month for Israel, and in particular, the city of Jerusalem! Golden Anniversaries are special. On June 10th, 1967, after 2,000 years of being in foreign hands, Jerusalem once again became the sovereign territory of Israel. The Six-Day War, known as The War of Miracles, liberated *Yerushalayim* back into the hands of its rightful covenant owners fifty years ago!

Yes it's true that according to the Hebrew calendar the official Independence Day, also known as the Reunification of Israel was celebrated on the 23rd of May. Thousands and thousands celebrated 'Jerusalem Day' festivities. Jerusalem Mayor Nir Barkat held a huge meet and greet reception at the Tower of David.

There was a parade, called *Rikudgalim*, with the

culmination of events taking place at the Western Wall. In Israel the activities took place in May, but what happened for six days in *June* fifty years ago, is vitally important to remember this month.

What's even more exciting is that 2017 was a Jubilee year, following a Shemitah (Shmita) year. This doesn't happen very often, and what a blessing for all of us to have been alive to celebrate this momentous season with Israel.

Fifty years ago, on June 5th, Israel began six days of fighting against Egypt, Syria, and Jordan. In only six days (the miracle stories of this war are renowned), Israel doubled its size, but the greatest victory was that Jerusalem was once again undivided. 1967 was also a Jubilee year. Jubilee years are special to God.

God instituted the Jubilee in Leviticus 25 that after seven cycles of Shmita, there is a Jubilee. Some debate whether the Jubilee is actually the 50th year, or the 49th, but regardless, it is a significant celebration. Jubilee largely deals with the land, and ownership of the land. That's why what happened in 1967 is so miraculous. In a year of Jubilee, with the supernatural help of Yahweh, *land* was restored to its rightful owners.

When other countries claimed the Promised Land for themselves, and didn't return that land to the rightful covenant heirs (in a year of Jubilee) GOD HIMSELF returned the land to his people. I just love that. God's laws and covenants supersede any human law.

Thousands of years earlier, God made a covenant with Abraham as to the appointed borders of the land promised to Abraham, Isaac, and Jacob. Thousands of years later, that physical land still belongs to descendants of these Patriarchs. One day, every square inch of the ancient boundaries will once again be possessed by his people.

God is serious about his Jubilee years. There is something remarkable that happens when the land 'rests' for twelve months. There is covenant blessing in the law of keeping the Jubilee as well as the Shmita year. In the 7th year (*every* seventh year), the Shmita, God declared that Jewish people should forgive one another of their debts.

1917 was also a Jubilee year. On November the 2nd of that year, foreign Secretary Arthur James Balfour wrote a letter to Baaron Lionel Walter stating Britain's support for a Jewish homeland in Palestine. A new national home for the Jewish people in Palestine.

The Zionist movement had 'sympathy' from 'His Majesty's Government'. That was one of the beginning days of God fulfilling the prophecy in Isaiah chapter 9. God hasn't forgotten the significance of the Jubilee, and neither should we.

1917 The Balfour Declaration
1967 The Six-Day War

It is important for us to know important dates in regards to Israel becoming a state again. It is also important for us to recognize the significance of the days and years of God's 'calendar' if you will.

In 2017, President Trump officially recognized Jerusalem as the capital of Israel. This was a huge declaration. While America itself isn't specifically mentioned in the Bible, making a stand for Jerusalem is significant. It was a Jubilee year.

Knowing the history of the Jewish people regaining their rightful land is important for any Christian or believer in Messiah. If we are to defend our stand with Israel, we must know how it came to be after so many years. We must also learn about the immense struggle it has been. But when God has an agenda, nothing can stop it.

Great Is Thy Faithfulness
נאמנות הוא גדול

David and I have been worship leaders for literally decades. We have sung thousands of hymns and songs throughout our lifetime. People often ask, "Do you have a favorite hymn or song?" The older I get, the more the words of the hymn 'Great Is Thy Faithfulness' resonate as favorites in my life.

As the words of that hymn continue to be a favorite, there is a spot in Israel that is *becoming* a favorite of mine. It's a spot that demonstrates God's perpetual faithfulness to his promises, the land of Israel, and the Jewish people. On our Holy Land portion of Zola Tours, we visit and explore the headwaters of the Jordan River.

Throughout our tours, we come in contact with, and travel beside all 156 miles of this ancient water source. Those on our trips have the opportunity to be baptized in the Jordan, just south of the Sea of Galilee. As we journey from Tiberius to the Dead Sea, we are able to view this river as it twists and turns throughout the Great Rift Valley. The Jordan is the main freshwater source that irrigates thousands of acres of agriculture throughout the county.

But my favorite section of this river? The northern headwaters. There's a line in a song my husband David has sung for years, *I Walked Today Where Jesus Walked*, that states, "And I saw the mighty Jordan roll..." If you were to view the Jordan south of the Sea of Galilee, that line wouldn't make any sense.

The river is quite calm down south. But up north, it's a completely different story. It's mighty. It's powerful. And it's an unforgettable experience to stand next to this robust source of life.

There are many freshwater springs that feed into the three 'headwater rivers' that become the Jordan. The Banias River, the Hatzbani River, and the Dan River (all fed from natural springs, and the melting snow from mountains in Lebanon and Mount Hermon). The word Jor-Dan itself means down from (*Jor*) the ancient city of *Dan*.

We have the privilege of walking through the Dan Nature Preserve on our way to view Tel Dan. Tel Dan is a gorgeous area where we not only explore an ancient city gate from the time of Abraham, but also the area of the Hebrew Tribe of Dan.

As a group, we traverse through this gorgeous preserve with paved trails and foot bridges that

147

spotlight the thunderous constant follow of the crystal clear *faithfulness of God*. In a desert land where water should be scarce, God continually provides.

When drought abounds throughout the Middle East, the mighty Jordan continues to flow. God has continued to keep his promises to his people. He's Yahweh-Yireh, our provider.

Just as the God we serve is unceasingly faithful to provide water to his people and land, he is faithful to provide our needs, *morning by morning*. All we have needed, his hand has provided. And he will never fail us.

This past March on our tour, I stopped on one of the bridges over the Dan River at a spot right before it becomes the Jordan. I stood in awe of the deafening roar of the steady flow. As gallons upon gallons of the purest water coursed beneath my feet, I knew I needed to capture that moment with my camera for all of you.

I paused that day for a photo and a reminder. No matter what happens in my life, God is faithful. The thunderous water beneath my feet was only a minute example of his infinite strength.

Be assured that whatever you may be walking through right now, the God of Abraham, Isaac, and Jacob is not weak. His power is unending. He is able to provide for your needs. Just as the water source for the Holy Land has never dried up, his resources for the needs in your life are constantly flowing.

He is our provider. *Great* is his faithfulness.

Todah Rabah
רבה תודה

Todah Rabah in Hebrew means thank you very much. I wanted to tell you, the reader of Aliyah of the Heart, *todah rabah*. Thank you for taking the time to read this book.

My heart's desire is that you will be drawn to the Holy Land in a way you never imagined. It's prophetic, you know. If you are a believer in our Jewish Messiah, he will call to you to help fulfill an ancient prophecy regarding his people and Israel.

Starting at Isaiah 60 verse 10, God is speaking through Isaiah about what Israel's future looks like in the times we are living in right now. We—you and I—are part of the 'foreigners' group. Through our support of Israel, we are literally fulfilling ancient prophecies. What incredible times we are living in!

"Foreigners will rebuild your walls, and their kings will serve you. Although I struck you in anger, yet in favor I will show you mercy. Your gates will always stand open; they will never be shut, day or night, so that the wealth of the nations may be brought into you, with their kings being led in procession...."

Every dollar spent in Israel is an investment into fulfilling prophetic scripture. Our prayer support (in addition to financial support) is literally building up the walls of protection for God's people and God's land.

As for the Hart household, we will always support Israel. My prayer through writing this book is that people will rise up across the Christian church to stand behind Israel, and to pray for the peace of Jerusalem on a daily basis.

I tell people across the country that there is only one city that will live on literally forever, and it's Jerusalem. We are told that Messiah himself will reign for 1,000 years from the very Jerusalem you are able to visit *today*! There isn't a single country in the world that can make that claim. That is why Israel is so incredibly important and special.

I'm not sure what our role will be when Jesus is reigning from Jerusalem, but we can be assured that we will have a part in the millennial reign of Christ on Earth. Then even better news—there will be a brand new Jerusalem built that we will all be able to live in.

There won't be a *new* New York City, not a 'new Paris', not even London. One city only. I hope in your lifetime that you will be able (at least once) to experience the most important city in the world.

Through every page in this book, I hope you have developed a deeper love and appreciation for the Holy Land. Just as God's Word is a 'living/breathing' work of God, so is his land. You can feel the electricity in the air. You can walk on streets that God himself in the flesh walked. You can be on a boat on the Sea of Galilee—and I like to think that possibly the same water molecules that Jesus walked on still 'float' in the water.

May this book be a 'starter kit' of sorts in your relationship with the Jewish people, our Jewish Messiah, and the land of Abraham, Isaac, and Jacob. I have given you tidbits of information. There's still so much more about this incredible land. My desire is that you will dig deeper and further to find out more about particular topics, locations, scriptures, and simply *all things Israel*.

Yes, God is calling the Jewish people from the north, south, east, and west to make Aliyah. He is also calling Christian believers to 'move their heart' to his land and people. Would you join us in *making Aliyah* with your heart?

God told Moses to tell Aaron how to bless the people of Israel in Numbers chapter six. It's called the Aaronic Blessing, and you will hear it spoken throughout Israel. I would like to leave you with this blessing. Shalom, my friend, and todah rabah for reading this book!

Here is a Hebrew interpretation of the Aaronic blessing. Praying this over you right now…

""YHWH will kneel before you presenting gifts and will guard you with a hedge of protection.

YHWH will illuminate the wholeness of his being toward you bringing order and he will give you comfort and sustenance.

YHWH will lift up his wholeness of being and look upon you and he will set in place all you need to be whole and complete."

Amen

אמן

ABOUT THE AUTHOR

Author of eight previous books, speaker and singer Kirsten Hart has been able to travel with some of America's premier Christian singing groups, including Re-Creation, Eternity, The Spurrlows, FRIENDS (the back-up group for Grammy Award winner Larnelle Harris), The Richard Roberts TV Singers, as a Praise and Worship Leader for International Crusades, on TBN's This Is Your Day telecast, as well as BET TV's Manasseh Jordan Show. Since moving to Branson, Missouri, she has been a part of DINO Kartsonakis' Christmas Spectacular Show, as well as his Tribute To The Titanic production.

She and her husband, David are the Co-Hosts for the Zola Levitt Presents Television program seen on the ABC Family Network, Daystar Network and hundreds of independent channels across the country. Along with the weekly television broadcasts, they also host two tours a year to Greece, Israel, and Jordan. For more information on their ministry with Zola Levitt Presents and the tours,
visit www.levitt.com.

She has had the amazing opportunity to work in television, speak and sing in churches across the world, and to be part of international crusades. She has shared her heart before thousands. She also counts it a privilege to have sung for Focus On The

Family and Compassion International events, Campmeetings, Statewide Conventions, and more.

Kirsten has spoken in churches and for Women's Ministry Events across the country for the past twenty years. She and her husband, Dave tour with a senior adult version of ReInventing You. They also have a music ministry and share about their heart for Israel.

Visit www.DavidandKirstenHart.com or www.KirstenHart.com to find out more.

If you are interested in helping people make Aliyah, would like a long or short-term opportunity to help with an incredible ministry in Israel, or simply want to find out more about what is happening daily in Israel, contact our friend Chaim Malespin at the Aliyah Return Center.

The Center is a place where Christians can get an in-depth experience living with, and helping both Jews and Arabs. We highly suggest (if God so lays it on your heart) to see what God is doing with this organization.

"Aliyah Return Center (ARC) is a branch of Return Ministries that likewise encourages Jews and Christians to work together to fulfill God's plans and purposes for Israel and the nations according to the Word of God. Now is the Time!

The ARC is a Bible-believing, prophecy-fulfilling ministry built on the foundation of love focused on building bridges between Jewish and Christian Communities and mobilizing the church to understand and embrace God's call to bless and serve Israel and the Jewish people. ARC is committed to standing with Israel and the Jewish people as ambassadors and advocates for Israel. We will continue to initiate and participate in events here in Israel and other nations in order to strengthen this unique and powerful bond between Jews and Christians - for such a time as this!

Aliyah is a crucial and central focus of Aliyah Return Center (ARC). We impart God's covenant love for Israel while revealing, teaching and mobilizing those to be a part of the prophetic 'Return and Restoration' of His Jewish People from the four corners of the earth to the land of Israel."

--Chaim Malespin

www.AliyahReturnCenter.com

COME TO ISRAEL WITH US!

Every Fall and Spring, we host tours to Israel. In the Fall, you can add a tour of Greece, and a Greek Islands cruise! After our Israel portion, add the extension to Petra! It truly is a trip of a lifetime! Contact www.levitt.com and click on the TOURS page for more information!

40396022R00088

Made in the USA
Middletown, DE
27 March 2019